THE STORY OF
AUSTRALIAN
ENGLISH

KEL RICHARDS is an Australian author, journalist and radio personality. Kel has written a series of crime novels and thrillers, episodes of the TV series *Murder Call*, and a number of language books, children's books and *The Dictionary of Australian Phrase and Fable* (2013).

Kel presented ABC NewsRadio's weekend afternoons, which included regular *Wordwatch* segments, until late 2010. Since 2010 Kel has been presenting Sydney radio station 2CH's Sunday night program.

THE STORY OF
AUSTRALIAN
ENGLISH

KEL RICHARDS

NEWSOUTH

A NewSouth book

Published by
NewSouth Publishing
University of New South Wales Press Ltd
University of New South Wales
Sydney NSW 2052
AUSTRALIA
newsouthpublishing.com

National Library of Australia Cataloguing-in-Publication entry
Author: Richards, Kel, 1946– author.
Title: The story of Australian English/ Kel Richards.
ISBN: 9781742232317 (paperback)
       9781742241906 (ePub/Kindle)
       9781742247168 (ePDF)
Subjects: English language – Dialects – Australia – History.
          English language – Australia – History.
          Australianisms.
Dewey Number: 427.994

Design Di Quick
Cover design Design By Committee, Josh Durham
Cover images Bigstockphoto.com

CONTENTS

1

WHAT IS AUSSIE ENGLISH?

The best place to begin is with a definition. 'Aussie English' is a dialect, and a dialect is a form of a language which is spoken only in one area – it is the speciality of the house in one local linguistic cafe. A dialect has words or grammar that are slightly different from other forms of the same language. That makes Aussie English a regional dialect of the English language.

Linguist David Crystal argues that most English usage in the world today consists of different dialects, and that so-called Standard English is largely restricted to Acts of Parliament and letters from your insurance company. In *The Stories of English* he writes: 'for every person who speaks Standard English, there must be a hundred who do not, and another hundred who speak other varieties as well as the standard.'

Standard English might be defined as the kind of English that all the users of different English dialects employ when communicating formally with each other in their best business suits. Standard English is what we encounter in official letters and reports, in the more self-important newspaper editorials, and in the language of global broadcasters such as the BBC and CNN.

There are obviously variations *within* Standard English. If two equally well educated professors both delivered formal papers at an international conference, one from England and one from America, they would differ in their pronunciation and their sentence construction while both speaking a type of Standard English.

But that's not what concerns us here. As David Crystal points out, the vast majority of English used around the world every day is (a) informal, and (b) a regional dialect of some sort.

The result is that Aussies do what most English users do: we shuttle between speaking (and writing) our own dialect (Aussie English) and Standard English. We'll use Standard English when we address a business meeting or write an email to a Canadian who might be baffled by Aussie words. But most of the time, among ourselves, we'll used bits of Aussie and bits of Standard English. Some people will use more of one than the other. Over a barbecue or a beer it's likely to be all Aussie. In the office it might be a mixture of both.

And this sort of 'mix and match' approach to English is what *most* users of the language do in most countries, most of the time.

That's why the language experts today talk about 'Englishes' instead of '*the* English language'.

By the way, what should we call our dialect? My publisher thinks it should be 'Australian English'. But I think it's more like an old jumper that's been through the wash a few times – shrinking it down to just 'Aussie'. (See chapter 16 for the way we shrink words.)

There are quite a few of these 'Englishes'. There is American English (with its many sub-dialects), Canadian English, New Zealand English, South African English and a wide range of English dialects spoken within the British Isles.

Some of the world's Englishes are strange and colourful. And some you may never have come across. For instance, there is 'Hinglish'. This is Indian English and comes from the collision of English and Hindi. Already 350 million Indians speak Hinglish.

Hinglish has a quaint, almost old-fashioned, formality in which people offer to 'do the needful', police 'nab' their man, 'miscreants abscond', youths engage in 'tomfoolery' and politicians say their opponents speak 'balderdash'. Hinglish is spiced with Hindi words, like 'pukka' for real, 'jungli' for uncouth, 'chappals' for sandals and 'chuddis' for underwear.

Then there are 'Singlish' and 'Manglish' – the first being the English dialect spoken in Singapore and the latter what they do to English in Malaysia.

And in this world of many Englishes there is our distinctive dialect – our very own dingo lingo.

Or is there?

Everyone agrees there once was an Aussie English – of that there is no doubt. The *Australian National Dictionary* records its (approximately) 10 000 contributions to the world family of Englishes. But does it still exist?

There is no shortage of doomsayers who claim that the regional dialect known as Aussie English is either dead or dying.

In *Lost for Words* (2006) Hugh Lunn writes:

> Once upon a time, Australians spoke a rich, evocative, expansive, euphonious, metaphoric, enthusiastic language. While this inventive tradition continues today with a few, a large slice of the Australian population now finds it simpler to constantly repeat the same few words and phrases, used ad infinitum in movies and on the American TV sitcoms which dominate the nation's evenings.

That gloomy view is simply wrong. It's a massive mistake that comes from misunderstanding what Aussie English is and how it works.

There are plenty of grumpy old men who'll agree with Hugh, and grumble over a beer that such rich and valuable words as 'bewdy', 'bottler' and 'ripper' have disappeared from the language. 'And when,' they sadly moan, 'was the last time anyone called you "cobber" or "digger"?'

I'll address Hugh's concerns in more detail in the last chapter of the book – that's where I'll pat Chicken Little gently on the shoulder and explain that the sky is not falling.

At this point I just want to explain the basic mistake that's being made here.

The doomsayers are confusing slang (the fastest changing component in any language) with the whole of Aussie English. This mistake is compounded by assuming that if slang changes it must be dying. In fact the very opposite is true: change is evidence of life, not death.

These unhappy people simply don't know what Aussie English really *is*. So, let me explain. Any English (any regional dialect, Aussie or otherwise) consists of *at least* four different components: (a) slang, (b) non-slang vocabulary, (c) accent and (d) grammar. So let's unpack each of those.

First, then, we look at slang.

What is slang? Well, it's that stuff you won't (as a rule) find in Acts of Parliament, insurance contracts or company reports. In a civil service memo Sir Humphrey might describe someone as a 'loquacious conversationalist'. But in slang we'd be more likely to say that the accused party will 'chew ya ear off.'

Here's an official dictionary definition of *slang*: 'language differing from standard or written speech in vocabulary and construction, involving extensive metaphor, ellipsis, humorous usage, etc., less conservative and more informal than standard speech, and sometimes regarded as being in some way inferior.' Mind you, that definition is certainly not written in slang. If I were to translate it into slang I might say that *slang* means 'muckin' around with words'.

Every English has its own slang – and slang tends to be that part of any English that changes fastest and changes most often. So if the grumpy old blokes no longer hear the slang words they used as kids, that just means that Aussie slang has moved on. It's not dying, just changing. (And, as I said, living languages change, not dead languages.)

The old grumps complain because they no longer hear an expression such as 'barmy as a bandicoot'. But when they were kids no one called Speedos 'budgie smugglers'. One slang term has died, another has been born. Aussie slang goes on. It changes, but it goes on. You'll find much of the Aussie slang of both the past and present recorded, and (where possible) explained in the pages that follow.

Second, there's our non-slang vocabulary.

This is something that all those whingers with a death wish for Aussie English never understand. They seem to be unaware that there are many fairly ordinary, non-slang words that are unique to Australia (or were born in Australia). For instance, in London you might live in a *flat*, in New York in an *apartment* or a *condo*, but only in Australia could you live in a *home unit*. That's proper English, not slang. But it's also an Australianism.

Backyard is hardly a slang word, but it is distinctively used in Australia and is just as much part of Aussie English as any comic slang term could be.

In just the same way those contrasting terms *in-ground pool* and *above-ground pool* are Australianisms. Any word or phrase originating in, or peculiar to, Australia is an Australianism – even if it's quite proper, and not the least bit slangy. For instance, all those names for our distinctive flora and fauna are Australianisms. And all the Aboriginal words that are part of Aussie English (from *barramundi* to *boomerang* and beyond) are the most Australian of Australianisms.

Only in Australia is bush bread (made from a simple flour and water dough, with or without a raising agent, cooked in the coals or in a camp oven) called *damper*. The word is recorded in this sense from 1825. It grew from an earlier (British) English word meaning 'something which takes the edge off your appetite' (see, it 'damps down' the appetite). But the application of *damper* to simple campfire bread happened only in Australia

– and it would be odd to claim that *damper* is slang. It is the normal, proper word for that kind of bread in Australia.

If you introduced your business partner to a visiting American as 'my offsider' the response might be a puzzled expression. *Offsider* is hardly a slang term, but it is an Australianism rarely heard outside this country.

Similarly, you could puzzle a visiting English friend by describing a careless young driver as a *hoon*. (Perhaps *hoon* still fits into the slang category, but *offsider* most definitely does not.)

The point is that we are largely unaware of our distinctive Aussie English for the same reason that a fish is unaware of being wet – because we are submerged in it.

These non-slang Aussie expressions tend to change rather more slowly than slang terms do – and are just as much part of what makes Aussie English distinctively Aussie.

Third, there is the Aussie accent. We'll look at this in detail in chapter 17, but the point here is that the way we speak is part of Aussie English. The accent has been described as both as flat as the Nullarbor Plain and as raucous as a kookaburra in full cry. The Australian accent is often said to be a spectrum of sound from 'broad Australian' at one end to 'cultivated Australian' at the other. But it's one spectrum, with a unifying vocal quality (especially in vowels) unlike any other place on the planet. Perhaps that sums up the Aussie accent: irritable vowel syndrome.

We have our own distinctive way of sliding sounds over the larynx, and it's part of what makes our language our own.

And finally, there is grammar.

This has two parts to it: morphology (meaning the shapes of words) and syntax (how the words are put together to make sentences). We don't know much about Aussie syntax at this stage, because little research has been done. However, in our universities there are linguists researching Australian grammar, so one day the picture will be clearer than it is now.

In the meantime, there are a few obvious things – such as the verbal tags some Aussies stick on the end of sentences (to let you know when the full stop is coming). 'Eh' is one such tag, with the meaning of 'is/isn't that so?'. 'So, you're a north Queenslander, eh. I was born up that way, meself, eh. But ya'd never know from the way I talk, eh.' Sometimes this tag is expanded into 'waddayareckon, eh?'.

Often no question is implied and the expression is little more than a verbal tic or spoken punctuation mark.

In some parts of Australia 'but' is added to the end of utterances in the same role ('It's a hot day, but') and sometimes the two are combined into the all-purpose tag 'eh but'. In this way Australians have made Victor Borge's 'phonetic punctuation' part of living speech. ('It's a clever thing to do, eh but!') In case you missed him, Victor Borge was a Danish comedian (died at a ripe old age in 2000) who included phonetic punctuation as one of his routines. This involved telling a story with all the punctuation marks (comma, full stop, exclamation mark, question mark and so on) spoken aloud as exaggerated vocal 'special effects'.

And then there's morphology: the shape of words. And the one thing Aussies like to do with words is shorten them. If after brekkie you go to the boozer with your mate Bazza the ambo, wearing his cardie, stay until the arvo, then drive home in his ute and chuck a U-ey, you'll find you're wading through a collection of classic Aussie diminutives. (More about them in chapter 16.)

So the sort of English spoken down-under consists of: slang, non-slang vocabulary, accent and grammar (and perhaps other bits I haven't thought of).

The point is that there's much more to Aussie English than just the slang.

This book tells the story of the birth, growth, history and current thriving life of that 'rich, evocative, expansive, euphonious, metaphoric, enthusiastic language' that Hugh Lunn refers to. It was born from four elements (as described over the next four chapters). Then it grew up in the bush and took off with explosive energy following the gold rushes of the mid nineteenth century. And, as the story unfolds you'll discover that it is as alive, inventive, colourful and vigorous today as ever. The doomsayers have got it completely wrong.

But for those who are still weeping into their beer, in the last chapter I'll have something to say about the future of Aussie English.

So now, let's go right back to the beginning, and get the story started.

WORD LIST

But before we do: each chapter in this book will end with a list of words appropriate to that chapter. There are, however, no particular words especially appropriate to this first introductory chapter. So, I thought I'd give you a list of eponyms – names that became words: famous Aussies whose names (or nicknames) became part of the language (some just for a time and some for a good deal longer).

BANJO pen name used by Andrew Barton Paterson (1864–1941) who wrote 'Waltzing Matilda', 'The Man from Snowy River' and heaps of other bush ballads. A top horseman, he took 'Banjo' from the name of one his favourite horses. Over time it was integrated with his family name, and he was spoken of as Banjo Paterson (although in the family he was always called Barty).

BENNELONG an Aboriginal man who gave his name to the peninsula in Sydney Harbour that is now home to the Sydney Opera House. He was captured on the orders of Governor Arthur Phillip in 1789. He lived for a time in a hut on what is now called Bennelong Point. He travelled with Phillip to England in 1792 where he was presented to King George III.

BIG FELLA, THE nickname given to Labor Premier of New South Wales Jack Lang (1876–1975). He was famously dismissed by the Governor of New South Wales, Sir Philip Game, in 1932 over his plan to suspend debt repayments to Britain during the Great Depression.

BLIND FREDDY 'even Blind Freddy could see that' is a colloquial expression used to indicate the highest degree of incompetence. Sidney J Baker, in *The Australian Language* (2nd edn, 1966) suggests the name may have come from a blind hawker who was well known in Sydney in the 1920s. While it's true that the earliest citation is from 1944, my guess is that 'Blind Freddy' was part of the spoken language long before that. And it's possible that the original Blind Freddy was an Englishman named Sir Frederick Pottinger. He was the man put in charge of catching bushranger Ben Hall (1837–65). As a new chum who knew nothing of the bush he kept failing in his attempts to trap the Hall gang – and Ben Hall's organising ability and knowledge of the bush meant that he ran rings around Sir Frederick. The sheer incompetence and clumsiness of Sir Frederick, I suggest, might have made him the original Blind Freddy.

BOYD, BEN gave his name to two small townships at Twofold Bay (on the south coast of New South Wales): Boyd Town and East Boyd. Ben Boyd (1803–51) ran a steamship service between Sydney, Twofold Bay and Hobart, and became a squatter and member of parliament.

BURKE AND WILLS, COVERED AS MUCH GROUND AS Robert O'Hara Burke and William John Wills died at Cooper Creek (in the heart of the outback) in 1861, attempting to find and map a north–south route across the continent of Australia. Their names have become a byword for geographical dyslexia.

CAPTAIN COOK, A rhyming slang for 'look' – chosen because of the role played by Captain James Cook (1728–79) in the European discovery of Australia.

CATTLE KING, THE Sir Sidney Kidman (1857–1953). Starting out as a stockman, by the time of his death he owned more cattle, and more grazing land, than anyone else on earth – a chain of cattle stations running from the Gulf Country down to the shipping and rail centre of Adelaide.

CAZALY!, UP THERE a cry of encouragement when the big men fly on the Aussie Rules paddock. Originally shouted out to legendary footy player Roy Cazaly (1893–1963) as he went for a high mark.

DON, THE Sir Donald Bradman (1908–2001), the greatest batsman cricket has ever known. His batting average in Test cricket was 99.94. Other batsmen struggle to do half as well!

FLYING PIEMAN, THE William Francis King (died 1874). He sold pies from a cart on the streets of Sydney and was noted for such feats as walking from Sydney to Parramatta and back in six hours for a bet.

FLYNN OF THE INLAND Presbyterian minister the Reverend John Flynn (1880–1951). Founder of the Australian Inland Mission and the Royal Flying Doctor Service. The expression *in like Flynn* is often said to refer to the amorous activities of Australian-born Hollywood movie star Errol Flynn, but I think it's just as likely to be a play on the name (and nickname) of Flynn of the Inland.

FURPHY a false or unreliable rumour. The earliest recorded use is 1915 among the diggers of the First World War. The firm of John Furphy & Sons operated a foundry at Shepparton in the late nineteenth century. One of their products was a water-cart. These water-carts were used by the Australian Army in World War I and (inevitably) became the place where diggers gathered and gossiped. The name Furphy was prominently printed on the back of each water-cart, and became the name for the unreliable gossip exchanged there.

GOYDER'S LINE a rainfall line dividing South Australia; above it the land was declared to be drought-prone and arid, while below it cultivation was said to be possible. Drawn by George Woodroofe Goyder in 1865 when he was Surveyor-General of South Australia.

HAPPY AS LARRY very happy. Sid Baker says that while we can't know for sure, it's possible this comes from an Australian boxer named Larry Foley (1847–1907). 'Happy as Larry' is first recorded in 1905, but was probably part of the spoken language well before that.

HINKLER, HUSTLING Bert Hinkler (1892–1933), pioneer aviator; made the first solo flight from England to Australia in 1928 in fifteen days, two and a quarter hours (which puts your Qantas flight to London on a 747 into perspective, doesn't it?).

HUME HIGHWAY from Sydney to Melbourne; named after Hamilton Hume (1797–1873), early Australian-born explorer of the parts of Australia not yet settled by Europeans.

JACKIE HOWE that sleeveless pullover worn by footy players is properly called a 'Jackie Howe' – named after Jackie Howe (1855–1922), the world's greatest blade shearer; his highest tally was shearing 327 ewes in seven hours and twenty minutes at Alice Downs (Queensland) in October 1892. Howe is said to have invented the garment to give him maximum freedom of movement while shearing.

LASSETER'S REEF an apparently mythical gold reef in Central Australia. Harold Bell Lasseter claimed to have found (and then lost again) this fabulous find. He died (probably of starvation) in 1931 while trying to re-discover its location.

LITTLE DIGGER, THE nickname of Australian Prime Minister Billy Hughes (1862–1952); famous mainly for changing political parties and for fighting a battle over conscription in the First World War.

MACQUARIE, LACHLAN Governor Lachlan Macquarie (1762–1824) seems to have named every second thing he bumped into after himself or his wife – hence the number of geographical features of New South Wales named 'Lachlan' or 'Macquarie' or 'Elizabeth'. His standard response, as he trotted around the colony, seems to have been to stop every so often and say, 'I name this after me'.

MR ETERNITY Arthur Stace (1884–1967) escaped from alcoholism when he became a Christian; he also became a footpath evangelist, writing the word *Eternity* (executed in beautiful copperplate in rain-resistant yellow crayon) on the streets of Sydney an estimated half a million times, from 1930 until shortly before his death. He intended his one-word sermon to be a question: 'Where will you spend eternity?' His word (in his style of writing) appeared on the Sydney Harbour Bridge in lights to mark the millennium, New Year's Eve 2000.

NED KELLY, AS GAME AS Australia's most famous bushranger, Ned Kelly (1855–80) was hanged after uttering the laconic words 'Such is life'. This, together with his wild exploits, gave us the expression 'as game as Ned Kelly'.

NELLIE MELBA, AS MANY FAREWELLS AS world-famous Australian-born soprano Dame Nellie Melba (1861–1931) was notorious for the many farewell tours she gave. Hence anyone who says goodbye and then hangs around is said to be making 'as many farewells as Nelly Melba'.

OUR GLAD legendary and much-loved musical comedy star Gladys Moncreiff (1892–1976).

PAVLOVA famous dessert (meringue topped with cream and fruit) invented in Australia (although New Zealand claims it!). In 1935, the chef of the Hotel Esplanade in Perth, Herbert Sachse, created the pavlova to celebrate the visit of the great Russian ballerina, Anna Pavlova, nine years earlier.

PHAR LAP, A HEART AS BIG AS courageous, game. Phar Lap is Australia's most famous racehorse, winning the Melbourne Cup in 1930; his heart has been preserved and is on display in the Melbourne Museum; from both the size of this amazing cardiac organ, and the horse's courage, comes the expression 'a heart as big as Phar Lap'.

SMITHY pioneer aviator Sir Charles Kingsford Smith (1897–1935); in 1927 he was pilot of the first flight across the Pacific (accompanied by Charlie Ulm and two Americans). He has given his name to Sydney Kingsford Smith Airport (and the aircraft he flew across the Pacific, the *Southern Cross*, is on display at Brisbane Airport).

YABBA real name Stephen Harold Gascoigne (1878–1942); legendary barracker from the Hill at the Sydney Cricket Ground; when a visiting English batsman had played at (and missed) a series of balls, Yabba bawled out in his gravelly, stentorian voice: 'Send him down a grand piano – see if he can play that!'

2

ENGLISH
ARRIVES

The English language arrived in Australia on 26 January 1788. At the time Mother England had rather more prisoners than she knew what to do with. They were like modern teenagers: picking up any spare cash around the place (because they were always short of pocket money), always raiding the fridge (in their case, the larder), and generally underfoot and in the way.

Mind you, it was pretty easy to become a prisoner in England in the late eighteenth century: poverty was rife and the laws were tough. Filling the prisons to overflowing were habitual prisoners (a good number being street-smart Cockneys from London), some political prisoners (notably the Irish) and an assortment of petty criminals from all over the country (locked up, often, when they went looking for a feed – perhaps poaching a rabbit on a noble lord's private parklands).

Then England carelessly lost her American colonies following a tea party in Boston in 1776. This deprived England of a distant land to which prisoners could be sent and forgotten about. So as the prisons burst at the seams, fresh waves of convicts were stored (as a temporary measure) on derelict ships, old hulks lying in various ports.

Then the question was: what to do with all these prisoners? This puzzle had Britain's leaders sitting around their White-hall clubs sipping their brandy in a grave and worried manner. Sir Joseph Banks, who had accompanied Captain James Cook on his Cook's Tour of the Great South Land in 1770, had the bright idea of shipping them off to Botany Bay. This struck the government of the day as a solution that would prevent riots on the hulks and stop the spread of contagious diseases.

So a total of 717 convicts (180 of them women) guarded by 191 marines and nineteen officers (under the command of Captain Arthur Phillip) were packed into a fleet of eleven ships and told that Botany Bay was 'more or less in that direction – off you go now'. And off they went.

And a very mixed bunch they were. Those convicts came from: Abingdon, Bodmin, Bristol, Bury, Chelmsford, Coventry, Croydon, Derby, Dorchester, Durham, East Grinstead, Exeter, Gloucester, Guildford, Hertford, Kingstone, Lancaster, Launceston, Lincoln, Liverpool, London, Lowth, Maidstone, Manchester, Monmouth, New Sarum, Northallerton, Ormskirk, Oxford, Plymouth, Poole, Preston, Reading, Sherborne, Shrewsbury, Southwark, Stafford, Taunton, Warwick, Wells, Wigan, Winchester, Worcester and York. The officers (and their families) that made up the New South Wales Corps were an equally mixed bunch.

Early in 1788 they made landfall in Botany Bay, didn't fancy the anchorage, and so sailed a little further up the coast to Sydney Cove in Port Jackson. Which is where they all tumbled ashore and ran up the flag on January 26th of that year.

The English settlers had arrived – and with them had come the English language.

But the diversity of their origins meant that it was an interesting sort of English language – full of various bits of slang from different parts of the country and an odd assortment of regional expressions.

Picture the situation: these new arrivals (housed at first in tents, then in primitive huts) on both sides of the Tank Stream that ran down to the harbour (roughly where Pitt Street is today), were unloading tools from the ships and clearing land. Both convicts and officers found themselves working side by side, day after day, with men and women from different parts of Britain. As they struggled to survive on a strange continent, surrounded by strange flora and fauna, they had another struggle to cope with: the struggle to understand each other.

Well, perhaps 'struggle' is putting it too strongly. But they certainly discovered that they didn't all use exactly the same words. They had different names for the same tools, or the same tasks. Some words were completely new to them, and others had different meanings. They were all products of the many British regional dialects and accents.

A map of the accents and dialects of Great Britain would look like a quilt of many small patches in a multitude of different colours put together from a basket full of odd-shaped scraps.

Sometimes you need only move from one county to the next to discover that the mode of speech has changed.

It was not just the Geordies and the Brummies, not just the Scousers and the Scots and the Cockney rhyming slang – it was also the scores of dialect and accent variations that existed in Britain (and still largely do) – differing from one valley to the next, and even from one town to the next.

And until these various dialect speakers from across King George's realm had been swept up by the British legal system, handpicked by the best judges in England, and deposited, first in a cell, and then in a sprawling open-air prison at the bottom of the world, they would *most likely never have heard another English dialect spoken!*

This was the eighteenth century – an era when the rich rode in carriages or on horseback, while the poor walked (if they travelled at all). At the time when the conductor was shouting 'All aboard for Botany Bay', most of the citizens of the British Isles would live and die without ever moving outside the county in which they were born. Many would never leave the village of their birth.

So for many (perhaps most) of the convicts (and the soldiers) the settlement in Sydney Cove was the place where they discovered that *other people had funny ways of speaking.* Old Sydney Town was where they discovered there were different ways of saying things from the ways they had grown up with.

If you had lived all of your life in a small village (where everyone spoke the same, had the same accent and used the same slang) and then were arrested (walking off a noble lord's private park carrying a sack containing several plump rabbits and a hare), once you arrived at Sydney Cove and started clearing land you were in for a shock. What you called a 'pick' the bloke beside you called a 'mattock' and the next bloke down the line called a 'grubbing-up tool'. In fact, unless you mixed with people called (in those unenlightened, politically incorrect times) Gypsies, or with Cockneys, you may have been unfamiliar with the word 'bloke'. (It was probably in those circumstances – disagreeing about the names of things – that the immortal line was first spoken: *'That's* not a knife! *This* is a knife!')

All those accents and assorted regional slang words must, inevitably, have alerted those first English settlers to the oddness of language.

CONVICT 1 (as he stumbles into Convict 2): 'Sorry me old china, I must've stumbled on the apples.'

convict 2: 'Speak English you Cockney idiot!'

CONVICT 1 (patiently): 'I said – sorry mate, I must have stumbled on the apples and pears.'

CONVICT 2: 'On the *what?*'

CONVICT 1: 'On the stairs.'

CONVICT 2: 'Oh, I see. Anyway, I'm not your mate. I'm not married to you, we're just working together, that's all. But you're you a decent bloke, so as far as I'm concerned you're my cobber.'

CONVICT 1: 'What's a cobber?'

(And so on – for several more pages of historically dubious dialogue.) But the point is that this process of British regional dialect words being adopted (and adapted) in Australia was one of the seeds from which Aussie English sprang.

Here is my suggestion: this discovery of unexpected variet-ies of English *was the birth of the Australian language – the birth of a distinctively Australian form of English*. Not, of course, that the word 'Australian' existed as a label yet. But Aussie English had begun long before there was a label for it. (There were several other early factors that pushed this embryonic Aussie English along – and we'll look at those factors in the next chapters.)

This very early component of Aussie English – regional English dialects – is still with us today. To this day there are words in Aussie English which come from a wide scattering of English regional dialect sources. Some of them have survived in Australia while disappearing from the living language in Britain. Others have survived in both places but with different meanings. Others have been changed or adapted in some way so that they no longer exactly resemble their dialect source word. Still others (mate is a good example) have remained the same in both places.

And it must have started at the very moment the colony was planted (if, in fact, it hadn't already begun on board the ships of the First Fleet on their way out to Australia's sunny shores).

Now all of this didn't happen, of course, in an instant – in that very first moment of the arrival of the First Fleet. But the process certainly *began* with that arrival.

An interest in language was born in that first convict colony (among both the convicts and their guards, and later among free settlers) with the discovery of regional dialects other than their own – the discovery that English was wider and more colourful than they had ever imagined. As these settlers started to use each other's regionalisms and slang words a new blended sort of English was being birthed – a blend that had not existed before.

This new, embryonic English included bits of Cockney rhyming slang, an Irish component, and regionalisms and collo-quialisms from across the British Isles. In addition, it incorporated (as we'll see in the new few chapters) some Aboriginal words, some words from a form of thieves' slang called 'flash talk', and some of the technical and official words that were part of a convict–military settlement.

But it was this exposure to the range of British regional dialects that was the first of these several components (I propose) that gave birth to the first tiny embryo that was to grow into Aussie English.

WORD LIST

Below are a few words from Aussie English that were either borrowed from, or adapted from, British regional expressions. Not all of the words on this list, of course, were present in 1788. Many of them arrived over the years as the colony expanded and free settlement replaced convict transportation. But all of them share a common source: British regional dialects.

BAIL UP was an English regional expression describing what you did with cows in order to milk them. As such the term was carried to Australia. But only in Australia did bail up become a description of how bushrangers (often convicts who'd fled to the rough freedom of the bush) treated their victims. Where an English highwayman might have ordered those he confronted to 'Stand and deliver', an Aussie bushranger shouted 'Bail up!' to the driver of the Cobb & Co coach. To this day, when the office bore traps you in the corridor so that you have to listen to his harangue an Aussie will say 'He bailed me up' where an Englishman would say 'He button-holed me'.

BILLY a pot in which to boil water (to make tea) over a campfire. It seems likely that the Scots have given us this one. There have been a number of theories as to its source over the years, but the truth seems to be that *billy* is a variant form of the Scottish dialect word 'bally', which in turn comes from 'bally-cog' meaning 'milk pail'. And a *billy* is bit like a smallish milk pail, so you can see how the word could be transferred in that way.

BLOKE an adult male. The *Oxford English Dictionary* says 'origin unknown' but then suggests that we might like to compare it to *loke*, the Romani (Gypsy) word for 'man'. And in the *Dinkum Dictionary* (2001) Susan Butler says the best guess is it comes from Shelta, a Romani language. In English it began by meaning an important man, or the man in charge. The vast Australian landscape flattened it into its current egalitarian meaning of 'everyman'. And then Aussies adapted it to other parts of speech, so that every code of football is now dominated by a culture called 'blokiness'.

BOOFHEAD now, sadly, a fading colloquialism meaning fool or simpleton. It comes from a north of England regional dialect word, *bufflehead* (meaning, literally, 'bullock head' or 'thick head'). Imagine bufflehead pronounced in a Yorkshire accent – it would sound something like 'booflehead'. And that's the word that was shortened in Australia (and only in Australia) to *boofhead*. The widespread use of this word is largely due to a comic strip called *Boofhead* written and drawn by RD Clark from 1939. It appeared in the Sydney *Daily Mirror* from May 1941 until Clark's death in 1970. Several collections of the strip were published as comic books in the 1950s. Boofhead's name was a description of his character. For instance, when the doctor asked: 'Did my medicine do you any good?', Boofhead replied: 'It was a wonderful remedy, doctor. I took three spoonfuls and my cough went. I rubbed four spoonfuls into my knee and it cured my rheumatism and I just left my mother at home using the rest of it to clean the silver.' (Pop artist Martin Sharp employed Clark's image of Boofhead as an Australian icon in a number of his paintings.)

DINKUM a word used by miners in Derbyshire to mean 'work' (especially hard work). And the way *dinkum* has changed over the years is typical of the way English regional dialect words have been incorporated into Aussie English. *Dinkum* went on meaning 'work' for some years, so that in *Robbery Under Arms* (1882) Rolfe Boldrewood has his central character Dick Marston say: 'It took us an hour's hard dinkum to get near the peak.' (He's talking about the hard work of driving a mob of cattle.) Later *dinkum* took on the adjective 'fair' – with the notion of 'a fair day's work for a fair day's pay'. Then this notion of honesty took over and became the main meaning of the word. Today *dinkum* means 'true; honest; genuine'. But it started life as a Derbyshire dialect word.

LARRIKIN a word used in Warwickshire and Worcestershire for a 'mischievous youth'. In the late nineteenth and early twentieth centuries *larrikin* became a much stronger word in Australia, meaning 'lout; hoodlum'. But then that harsh sense seemed to soften again. My own memory is that in my childhood *larrikin* was a word of gentle, even affectionate, rebuke.

NONG means an idiot. It seems to have begun life somewhere in Yorkshire as the word *nigmenog*, meaning 'very silly fellow'.

Over time this became 'nig-nog' and then 'ning-nong' and then simply 'nong'. Thus does Aussie English grow words out of English dialect soil.

PADDOCK what Aussies call a *paddock* the rest of the world seems to a call a 'field'. But *paddock* was originally a British word meaning a 'small field or enclosure'. In Australia a paddock is rarely small (in fact, it can cover as much land area as a city) and is often not enclosed (at least in the outback). The original English meaning dates from the sixteenth century, and the distinctively Australian variation from early in the nineteenth.

SHEILA the female equivalent of 'bloke'. This is another we seem to have borrowed from the Irish. The earliest citation in the *Oxford English Dictionary* suggests that it was originally one of a pair: you would speak of 'Sheila and Paddy' – these being the two most common Irish Christian names. But, somehow, in Australia 'sheila' lost its capital letter, and lost contact with Paddy – being paired with 'bloke' as the generic terms for male and female.

SKERRICK the smallest amount, a 'scrap'. This one quite possibly comes from *scuddick*, a northern English dialect word, and was originally used only in a negative context, as in 'not a skerrick'. Nowadays we seem to have developed a positive construction as well, as in 'Is there any of that cake left?' 'Just a skerrick.'

WATTLE many of the species of *Acacia* that were used for an ancient building technique, used in parts of England and by the early settlers, and known as *wattle and daub*, came to be called *wattles*. The technique involved rods or stakes of wood driven into the ground, with twigs or branches woven between them (wattled) to form walls. These walls were often caked (daubed) with mud or clay to make them wind and weather proof.

<u>**YOUSE**</u> plural form of 'you'. The *Australian National Dictionary* suggests this one probably came out with the Irish. The *AND* lists it as the dialectal plural form of 'you' and cites examples from Ireland, Australia and the United States.

3

THE FLASH
LANGUAGE

I am old enough to remember, as a child, hearing older aunts and uncles (and other assorted adults) speak about 'the convict stain'. This expression made modern Australia's birth as a convict colony sound like that embarrassing thing the dog did on the carpet in the front room. In those days convict ancestry was regarded as a blot on the escutcheon. If you had any convict branches in your family tree you reached for the bottle of Wite-Out and got rid of them. But times have changed, and today Australians trek through their family history hoping to find a convict or two.

Those convicts are important to the story of our language because not all convicts were political prisoners, or innocent yokels who'd been caught doing a bit of poaching. In fact the majority were professional crooks – and they had their own language. It was a special type of slang that was meant to work as a kind of code, so that they could speak to each other in the presence of honest citizens (even in the presence of magistrates or thief takers) and not be understood. Their coded slang meant they could utter apparently innocent (or incomprehensible) remarks that would convey a sinister meaning only to those in the know.

This language of the criminal underworld was called, by proper persons, 'thieves' cant'. And just in case you haven't come across this expression before, *cant*, in this context, means (according to the dictionary) 'the words, phrases, etc., peculiar to a particular class'. But the thieves themselves called this special slang they spoke 'the flash language'.

So, when hundreds of professional crooks arrived on the sunny shores of Sydney Cove the flash language came with them. (And this was even before there were tabloid newspapers to print horrified headlines and call for longer sentences.)

Now at this point I need to introduce you to a gentleman named James Hardy Vaux (he seems to have pronounced his surname to rhyme with 'hawks').

Vaux was born in the village of East Clandon, in Surrey, on 20 May 1782. This means that he was only six years old (well, almost six) when the British flag was being run up over the new convict colony down-under. So he missed the boat, as it were, when the First Fleet was assembled. But he quickly made up for this omission.

According to his own account Vaux came from a good family and was given a number of opportunities, when in his teens, to adopt an honest profession. But being a singleminded young man he avoided all these temptations to go straight, and devoted himself to a life of crime. He became a swindler and a pickpocket, known to his confederates as 'The Count' (he used the name Le Compte de Vaux in a number of his swindles).

Because of his diligent application to a career of crime, James Hardy Vaux managed to get himself caught stealing a handkerchief in April 1800 (a month before his eighteenth birthday). He was convicted at the Old Bailey in London and transported to the penal colony of Botany Bay (it took London some years to work out that the colony was actually some miles to the north at Sydney Cove) for seven years. He arrived here to begin his sentence in 1801.

But that was just the beginning. By unswerving devotion to ham-fisted dishonesty Vaux managed to get himself transported to Australia no fewer than three times. This alone should earn him a little footnote in Australian history. But while he was here he did something rather more important for our story: he compiled a *Vocabulary of the Flash Language* – recording how London underworld slang was being used (and was flourishing) in the young settlement.

This little dictionary (of around 750 headwords) he put together in 1812. At the time he was at the convict station at Newcastle – called, in those days, 'the hell of New South Wales'. Vaux had been sent to Newcastle as a kind of second level of punishment for having returned to his old thieving ways. And he didn't steal from just anyone, he stole from Judge Advocate Ellis Bent (which suggests he suffered from kleptomania or stupidity or an astonishing degree of self-confidence).

Vaux claimed to have compiled his little dictionary during his 'solitary hours of cessation from hard labour'. Well, he *may* have been forced to do hard labour on occasions, but as one of the few convicts who was literate he was most often employed in the commander's office on clerical duties.

Seven years later Vaux wrote his *Memoirs*. The full title of his book was: *Memoirs Of The First Thirty-Two Years Of The Life of James Hardy Vaux, A Swindler and Pickpocket; Now Transported, For The Second Time, And For Life, To New South Wales, Written By Himself.* (Ah, they don't write titles like that anymore!)

The book is dedicated to Captain Thomas Thompson, the commander of the Newcastle convict station, who (says Vaux) encouraged him to write this account of his life. This manuscript came into the hands of the new Judge Advocate of the colony, Baron Field. Perhaps Vaux himself sent it to the judge, or perhaps Captain Thompson did. At any rate Field did some editorial work on Vaux's material, and then sent it to his own London publisher, John Murray – and when it appeared in print, in 1819, it contained (as an appendix at the back) Vaux's *Vocabulary of the Flash Language*.

Vaux himself now disappears from our radar, since it's his little dictionary that interests us. However, I should mention that after completing *another* prison term in 1841 James Hardy Vaux disappears completely from the historical record. He walked out of prison on 18 August 1841, and off the pages of history. Did he die shortly after his release? Or did he, at the age of fifty-nine, finally succumb to the temptations of middle-class respectability? That's one of the little mysteries of history.

So, turning to the *Vocabulary* itself, what did the flash

language contribute to Aussie English? The answer appears to be: a number of words we think of as being very Australian.

For a start there is that archetypal 'Waltzing Matilda' word *swag*. Here's Vaux's definition in full:

> **swag** a bundle, parcel or package; as a *swag* of snow etc. The *swag* is a term used in speaking of any booty you have lately obtained, be it of what kind it may be, except money, as 'Where did you *lumber the swag?*' That is, 'Where did you deposit the stolen property?' *To carry the swag* is to be the bearer of the stolen goods to a place of safety. *A swag* of anything signifies emphatically a great deal. To have *knap'd a good swag* is to have got a good booty.

(Some words in that definition may need explaining: *snow* means 'clean linen from a washerwoman's hands'; *to lumber* any property is to deposit it somewhere for security; and *to knap* something is to steal it.)

From that beginning it's possible to see how the word *swag* grew in the Australian climate until it came to have its classic Aussie meaning: 'a bundle or roll carried across the shoulders or otherwise, and containing the bedding and personal belongings of a traveller through the bush' (so says the *Macquarie Dictionary*).

In his definition Vaux is already giving us two meanings: both stolen property (the thief's booty) or, more generally, 'a bundle, parcel or package'. As itinerant bush work replaced theft as a way of earning a living that second meaning took over from the first, leading us (eventually) to the 'jolly swagman' of Banjo Paterson's classic bush ballad.

In his 1907 short story 'The Romance of the Swag', Henry Lawson described what you might find in most swags: 'The swag is usually composed of a tent "fly" or strip of calico (a cover for the swag and a shelter in bad weather ...), a couple of blankets, blue by custom and preference ... and the core is composed of spare clothing and small personal effects.' (And because the blankets were most commonly blue the swag was also known as a *bluey*.) Thus Vaux's swag became a very special kind of bundle, parcel or package which then gave rise to forms such as 'swagman' and 'swaggie'.

That's an example of how a bit of the flash language of the London criminal class entered and influenced Aussie English. And it's not the only bit.

Cove is a word that is probably disappearing from Aussie English today, but it once played a significant role, more or less as a synonym for 'bloke'. And *cove* is another of Vaux's flash words:

> **cove** the master of the house or shop is called *the Cove*; on other occasions, when joined to particular words, as a *cross-cove*, a *flash-cove*, a *leary-cove* etc., it simply means a man of these several descriptions; sometimes, in speaking of any third person, whose name you are either ignorant of, or don't wish to mention, the word *cove* is adopted by way of emphasis.

Here a 'cross-cove' means a crook (not to be trusted), a 'flash-cove' is someone who is sharp (who knows what's going on), and a 'leary-cove' is someone who is vigilant, suspicious or cunning. By the way, *leary* over time became *lairy* – and as the word changed so did the meaning: by the end of the nineteenth century someone who was *lairy* was flashily dressed.

Meanwhile, *cove* had entered Aussie English – first meaning 'the boss' and then any adult male. In the early days the officer in charge of a gang of convicts was 'the cove'. Then among bush workers, the boss of a sheep station was 'the cove'. The landlord of an inn or pub could also be called 'the cove'. From the citations in the *Australian National Dictionary* it appears that by 1830 (or thereabouts) the meaning had broadened from just the boss to all the blokes.

To this day we can use surviving bits of the flash talk in our ordinary conversation without even knowing we're doing so. Take, for instance, Vaux's entry on the expression *awake* or *wake-up*:

> **awake** an expression used on many occasions; a thief will say
> to his accomplice, on perceiving the person they are about to
> rob is aware of their intention, and upon his guard, *stow it*, the
> *cove's awake*. To be *awake* to any scheme, deception, or design,
> means generally to see through or comprehend it.

So when you say to someone in the office (who's trying to pull the wool over your eyes): 'Come off it! I'm *awake-up* to you!' you're speaking the language Mr Vaux and his convict colleagues introduced to this country. (And by the way, as you can see here, *stow it*, meaning 'drop the subject, forget about it', is another bit of flash talk picked up by Aussie English.)

Such is the influence of the flash language that arrived with the First Fleet, and kept on coming with each fresh shipload of convicts, until transportation was finally abandoned for good in 1852.

At the very least we can say that flash talk joined British dialect words in imprinting its linguistic DNA on the embryonic language that was to become Aussie English.

WORD LIST

Here are some more entries from Vaux's *Vocabulary of the Flash Language*. Some are included because they provide further evidence for the early influence of the flash talk on our linguistic culture, and some just because they're fun. The definitions are given in the words of James Hardy Vaux.

BANG-UP a person whose dress or equipage is in the first style of perfection is declared to be *bang up to the mark*.

BARKING-IRONS pistols.

BASH to beat any person by way of correction.

BLOW THE GAFF a person having any secret in his possession, or a knowledge of any thing injurious to another, when at last induced from revenge, or other motive, to tell it to the world and expose him publicly is then said to have *blown the gaff* upon him.

BOLT to run away from or leave any place suddenly.

CADGE to beg.

CHEESE IT the same as *stow it*.

CHUM a fellow prisoner in a jail, hulk, etc.

CLEANED OUT said of a gambler who has lost his last stake at play.

CROAK to die.

DING to throw, or throw away; particularly any article you have stolen, either because it is worthless, or that there is a danger of immediate apprehension. To *ding* a person is to drop his acquaintance totally; also to quit his company, or leave him for the time present.

DOLLOP a large quantity of any thing.

DUDS women's apparel in general.

FENCE a receiver of stolen goods.

FLAT in a general sense any honest man or *square cove*, in opposition to a *sharp* or *cross-cove*.

FLY vigilant; suspicious; cunning; not easily robbed or duped; a shopkeeper or person of this description is called a *fly cove*.

GALLOOT a soldier.

GAMMON flattery; deceit; pretence.

GRAB to seize; apprehend; take in custody.

GRUB victuals of any kind.

HIS-NAB him or himself; a term used by way of emphasis when speaking of a third person.

JOB any concerted robbery, which is to be executed at a certain time is spoken of by the parties as *the job*.

KICK a sixpence, when speaking of compound sums only, as *three and a kick* is three and sixpence.

LAG a convict under sentence of transportation.

LARK fun or sport of any kind.

LUSH (1) to drink; speaking of a person who is drunk they say *Alderman Lushington is concerned* or he has been *voting for the Alderman*; (2) beer or liquor of any kind.

MUG the face; a *queer mug* is an ugly face.

NIB a gentleman or person of the higher order.

OUT-AND-OUT quite; completely; effectually.

PLANT to hide or conceal any person or thing is termed *planting* him or it.

PLUMMY right; very good; as it should be.

PUSH a crowd or concourse of people, either in the streets, or at any public place of amusement.

PUT-UP AFFAIR any pre-concerted plan or scheme to effect a robbery etc., undertaken at the suggestion of another person who, possessing a knowledge of the premises, is competent to advise the principal how best to proceed.

QUEER bad; counterfeit; false; unwell in health.

QUEER IT spoil it.

QUID a guinea.

QUOD a jail.

RUM good, in opposition to *queer*.

SCHOOL a party of persons met together for the purpose of gambling.

SHARP a gambler or person professed in the arts of play; a cheat or swindler.

SLOP tea.

SLY any business transacted, or intimation given, privately ... is said to be *done upon the sly*.

SNOOZE to sleep.

SQUARE all fair, upright and honest practices are called the square in opposition to the cross.

SWELL a gentleman; but any well-dressed person is emphatically a *swell* or *a rank swell*.

TANNER a sixpence.

TIP to give, pay, or bribe.

TRAPS police officers, or runners, are properly so called; but it is common to include constables of any description under this title.

TRY IT ON to make an attempt ... where success is doubtful.

WACK a share or equal proportion, as *give me my wack*, that is, my due part.

YARN *yarning* or *spinning a yarn* is a favourite amusement among flash-people; signifying to relate their various adventures, exploits and escapes to each other. This is most common and gratifying among persons in confinement or exile, to enliven a dull hour, and probably exciting a secret hope of one day enjoying a repetition of their former pleasures.

4

NATIVE TONGUES

Discovering the range of British dialects thrust together in the convict colony would (I am arguing) have made those early settlers very aware of language (even, in a sense, very sensitive to language). Finding out that there are different names for the same thing gives people a choice in which word to use, and makes them aware of that choice – aware of words. Added to this was the flash language, which often involved playing games with words – and you can't play with words without being aware of words.

The combined experience would have been as startling as being smacked in the back of the head with a very large dictionary (or possibly a thesaurus).

And there was yet another factor pushing the English-speaking settlers in the direction of awareness of words and verbal invention: namely, all the new things for which they didn't (as yet) have names.

The settlers were surrounded by decidedly odd flora and fauna for which the English language had no words. Try to imagine the first of the newcomers to spot a platypus. He probably found himself able to do nothing but utter an inarticulate gasp of 'Look at that ... that ... that ... *thing!*'.

To help them out in naming these things, they quite often turned to the locals.

Although these new settlers denied local tribes access to lands they had used for thousands of years, the relationship between the two groups was not unremittingly hostile. Governor Arthur Phillip made an effort to study and understand the traditional inhabitants of the Sydney area. An Aboriginal man named Bennelong was, on Phillip's orders, captured and brought to Sydney Cove for observation in 1789. He escaped in 1790 but later returned to the settlement. A hut was built for him on the eastern side of what is now Circular Quay in 1791.

In addition to such official attempts at contact (and study and communication), unofficial and informal contact was being made constantly. A gang of working convicts, or a squad from the New South Wales Corps, would come across a group of curious Aboriginal people and attempts would be made by both groups at communication. Both sides were puzzled by the other, and both curious.

Some of the leaders of the settlement (including David Collins, Deputy Judge Advocate with the First Fleet, John

Hunter, captain of the First Fleet ship HMS *Sirius*, and Governor Phillip himself) collected glossaries of Aboriginal words. This makes it clear that the settlers were slowly learning local names for the odd animals and plants around them. And not just plants and animals either. Names for weapons, dwellings and some cultural terms were also recorded.

For instance, *boomerang* is first recorded as early as 1790, perhaps because the settlers found the object so intriguing – it was like no weapon they had ever come across before. The same year gives us *nulla nulla* (hardwood club) and *gunyah* (hut or dwelling). And a few years later *woomera* is recorded as the name for a spear-thrower.

All of these are Dharuk words. The Dharuk were the Aboriginal people living in the immediate vicinity of the first settlement and, in consequence, there are more Dharuk words in Aussie English than from any other Aboriginal language. The fact that there were a large number of different languages spoken by different Aboriginal peoples was something it took the English settlers a while to come to terms with.

Which brings us to the interesting story of *kangaroo*. This word was collected by Captain Cook and Sir Joseph Banks in what is now north Queensland in 1770. The *Endeavour* had struck a reef and had to be beached for repairs (at the mouth of what is now called the Endeavour River).

While the repairs were going on, Banks and his assistants attempted to collect some Aboriginal names for local animals and plants. They did this with sign language – much pointing, raising of eyebrows, quizzical expressions, and asking 'What's that?' This is obviously a very dodgy method. But Banks, who was no fool, realised this, and tried to allow for possible errors. Banks and two or three others each carried out this procedure separately and compared their lists. He concluded that, 'those [words] in which all the lists agreed, or, rather, were contradicted by none, we thought ourselves morally certain not to be mistaken in'.

From this effort came a glossary which Arthur Phillip brought with him when he sailed for Botany Bay. But it did not at the time occur to anyone that Aboriginal people at one end of Australia spoke a quite different language from Aboriginal people at the other.

One of the words Banks had collected in north Queensland was *kangaroo* – meaning exactly what you know it means. Or do you want a definition? All right, the *Macquarie Dictionary* will supply one: 'any of the largest members of the family Macropodidae, herbivorous marsupials of the Australian region, with powerful hind legs developed for leaping, a sturdy tail serving as a support and balance, a small head, and very short forelimbs'. Happy now?

At any rate, the First Fleet settlers, when trying to converse with the local Aboriginal people, pointed to kangaroos hopping around and said *kangaroo* (and they probably said it loudly, several times – that being the standard way of communicating with people who speak a different language). Well, the locals (quite reasonably) assumed this was an English word meaning (more or less) 'animal'.

Captain Watkin Tench recorded in his journal seeing an Aboriginal group looking at some sheep in an enclosure and repeatedly crying out, 'Kangaroo! Kangaroo!' This put Tench on the right track, and he eventually worked out that the local word for kangaroo was *patagaran*. But by then *kangaroo* had stuck, and they've been kangaroos ever since.

As a side issue, it's probably worth getting rid of the old myth that when Sir Joseph Banks asked a north Queensland Aboriginal group 'What's that?' they replied 'Kangaroo' meaning 'I don't know' (or something equally silly). The experts now seem to think that the Queensland locals really did give Banks the proper name for the animal, but that the name they used was not the generic name for *all* kangaroos – rather it was local name for a specific kangaroo (namely, the type now known to scientists as *Macropus robustus*).

But despite such muddles Aboriginal words were entering English, and taking their place alongside British regional dialect terms and flash words in shaping the new baby that would grow up to become Aussie English.

Those early settlers were busy with their notebooks: *corroboree* was recorded in 1790 as meaning 'an Aboriginal dance ceremony'. Much later the word was borrowed and applied to any large, noisy gathering. *Coo-ee* was not recorded until 1824 as a call used in the bush to attract attention over a distance, used by Aboriginal people and picked up from them by the early white colonists; the first part of the word is long and the second part has a rising tone ('coooooo-*whee!*'). Again over time the meaning of *coo-ee* was extended so that it came to refer to an imprecise measurement of distance: anything or anyone that can be seen or heard is *within coo-ee*.

Koala is another Dharuk word. It was first recorded in 1798 (although the spelling wobbled around for a few years until it settled into its familiar form). The *kookaburra* got its proper name a little later, in the 1830s. Before that settlers called it the 'laughing jackass' and accused it of mocking their efforts at carving a mini-European settlement out of the bush.

As early as 1793 the Dharuk word *kurrajong* had entered English as the name for a useful fodder plant. And it was an Aboriginal language that gave us the name *bindi-eye* for *Soliva pterosperm*a, a low-growing plant with small spiky burrs which are painful when trodden on with bare feet.

Later *bindi-eye* was shortened to just *bindi*. This is because when you're hopping around, howling, and pulling burrs out of your feet, you need a short answer to the question: 'What's up with you?' I mean, you don't want to say, 'I just trod on a soliva pterosperma!!!', do you? Of course not! Much easier to say, 'I just trod on a rotten bindi! The lawn's full of them!'

The Aboriginal name for the nicest eating fish in the world, the *barramundi*, is recorded as part of English from 1864. In other words, the process of borrowing Aboriginal words that began in 1788 continued – and it continues to this day.

Another 'Waltzing Matilda' word, *billabong*, was recorded by explorer Thomas Mitchell in 1836. And that mythical creature the *bunyip* was borrowed from another Aboriginal language in the 1840s.

The point of all this for the story of Aussie English is that you can't use a *new* word without being aware of words. And that's part of what was happening to the linguistic embryo that was to grow (in time) into Aussie English. A new type of English was emerging from an awareness of words (an alertness towards words) that came from all these sources: the British dialect words, the flash words, and the borrowed Aboriginal words.

At this point another short excursion is necessary to make

the point that some words that are commonly assumed to be of Aboriginal origin aren't. Here are four examples: piccaninny, bandicoot, emu and goanna. Those look to many people as if they must have started life as Aboriginal words – but none of them did.

Piccaninny (meaning a child, especially an Aboriginal child) comes from the Portuguese *pequenino* meaning 'very little'. *Piccaninny* first appeared in the seventeenth century in that part of the West Indies visited by the Portuguese. From there it entered the English language with the meaning of 'native child' and it was the English who brought the word to Australia. Here its meaning was extended metaphorically. So the first, faint light of dawn was called 'piccaninny dawn', and something that was only a short walk away was said to be 'only a piccaninny distance away'.

There is a similar story behind *bandicoot* (a digging, rather rat-like marsupial). In this case the word comes from the days of the Raj, like many others being picked up during the days of the British rule of India. It comes from a Telugu word meaning 'pig-rat' and was first applied to a large Indian rat (described as being as large as a cat and very destructive). When ex-Indian Army chappies settled in the eastern Australian colonies the word came with them, and they applied it to the digging, sharp-snouted marsupial mentioned above (scientific name *Perameles nasuta*), and by extension to its many relatives across the country.

Emu is another word that comes from the Portuguese. It was first applied to the crane, later to the ostrich, and then to various birds of ostrich-like appearance. Here it was applied to the large, flightless Australian bird *Dromaius novahollandiae*.

(The last bit of that Latin name means 'New Holland' – reminding us that this was one of the names given to this continent before 'Australia' was finally, and officially, settled upon.)

And *goanna* is a corruption of the Spanish word *iguana* – I guess because both are large lizards.

But these oddities are the exceptions.

For the most part, as the years rolled by English-speaking settlers named the local oddities by trying to find out the Aboriginal name for whatever it was they were looking at. Which is how the *bilby*, the *yabby*, the *waratah*, the *mallee*, the *budgerigar* (later shortened to 'budgie'), the *dingo* and countless other bits of Aussie flora and fauna were named.

English-speaking settlers also (not always, but quite often) turned to Aboriginal languages for help with placenames. For instance, the second English settlement in Australia (established in November 1788) was up the river that flowed into Port Jackson from the west. The place was first named Rose Hill (after a British Treasury official) but a few years later renamed *Parramatta* – the local Aboriginal name, which is usually said to mean 'head of the waters'.

This practice ended up leaving the map of Australia scattered with Aboriginal words: from *Boggabri* to *Currabubula* to *Mangurup* to *Oodnadatta* to *Wagga Wagga* (more on this in chapter 19.)

This, then, was the third element that imprinted its DNA on the linguistic baby that was to grow up into Aussie English. So far we've identified three of the four linguistic grandparents of Aussie English, and only one remains. We'll come to it in the next chapter.

WORD LIST

Here is a small sampling of some of the other Aboriginal words that made their way (over the years) into Aussie English. Some of these words were once more common than they are now, and others only ever had a regional circulation (there'll be more about regional variations in Aussie English in chapter 19).

BOGONG a brown moth (from an Ngayawung word).

BOMBORA a wave which forms over a submerged offshore reef or rock (probably from a New South Wales Aboriginal language).

BOOBOOK an Australian owl (from the Dharuk word *bug bug* – both the Dharuk original and the English adaption seem to imitate the two-note call of the owl).

BOONDIE a stone (from a Western Australian Aboriginal language).

BRIGALOW certain types of *Acacia* trees (possibly from the Kamilaroi word *burigal*).

COOLIBAH a species of gum tree (from *gulubaa*, from Kamilaroi and related languages).

COONDIE a stone (from a Western Australian Aboriginal language).

CURRAWONG an Australian bird with predominantly grey or black plumage (from *garrawang*, from Jagara and neighbouring languages).

GIBBER a stone or rock (from the Dharuk word *giba*).

GIDGEE scrub (from *gijir*, from Wiradhuri and related languages).

GIN an Aboriginal woman or wife (from the Dharuk word *diyin*).

GONNIE a stone, especially one small enough to throw (from a Queensland Aboriginal language).

GOOLIE another name for a small stone (from a New South Wales Aboriginal language).

JACKAROO a young man working on a sheep or cattle station (from *jaggara*, an Aboriginal name for a wandering white man living in the bush).

JARRAH the tall trees of the south-west of West Australia (from a Nyunga word).

KYLIE the Nyunga (Western Australian) Aboriginal word for a boomerang.

MIN MIN will-o'-the-wisp; a mysterious outback light (from a Queensland Aboriginal language).

MULGA can refer to several plants of the genus *Acacia*; or to the bush (the outback) generally (from the Yuwaalaraay word *malga*).

PADEMELON a small, compact-bodied wallaby (probably from the Dharuk word *badimalion*).

PERENTIE the largest goanna (or monitor lizard) found in Australia (apparently from the South Australian Diyari word *pirindi*).

QUANDONG a shrub or small tree found in the dry country of southern Australia (from the Wiradhuri language).

RONNIE a stone, especially one small enough to throw (from a South Australian Aboriginal language).

WADDY a stick of wood (from the Dharuk *wadi*).

WALLABY any of the smaller kangaroos are so called (from the Dharuk word *walaba*).

WILLY WILLY a whirlwind (from the Yindjibarndi word *wili wili*).

WOBBEGONG a slow-moving, bottom-dwelling shark (probably from a New South Wales Aboriginal language).

WOMBAT a thick-set burrowing marsupial (from the Dharuk word *wambat*).

YAKKA work, especially hard work (from the Yagara word *yaga*).

YONNIE a stone, especially one small enough to throw (from a Victorian Aboriginal language).

5

CONVICT WORDS

The fourth factor that went into breeding the baby that became Aussie English is one that (given the nature of the first English settlement) you might expect to play a role – the convict–military nature of the colony. Having a sergeant major bellowing military jargon at you from dawn till dusk is likely to drive it into your skull and make it part of your own lingo.

Here are a few examples.

If you grazed animals in Britain you would do so on a *farm*, and that would make you a farmer. In America your property would be called a *ranch*, and you would be a rancher. But in Australia the man whose rural activity consists mainly of raising either sheep or cattle (or both) is a called a grazier and his property is called a *station*. So why a station? Why not a farm or ranch?

The name comes from the military use of the word. The nature of armies (and navies, for that matter) is to be on the move. If they are not properly mobile they are not of much use. What any good general wants to discover when he arrives at his base after a good night's sleep is that his troops have risen early, enjoyed a full English breakfast, and are now on the move.

But there are places that act as such bases – places they move *from* to the field of action. In such places the army is not moving – it is stationary – and so such places (with their barracks and mess halls) were called *stations*. Fairly logical, really.

Now when you have an army, such as the New South Wales Corps, whose main task is to guard convicts, then the place where both will be garrisoned will be called a 'convict station' – as indeed it was. Basically, such a station was an outpost of the colonial government.

From this common usage it seems it was only a short step to calling a tract of grazing land that had a discernible centre of occupation a *station*. This usage is recorded in the *Australian National Dictionary* from 1820. Then from 1839 the legal entitlement to the use of a tract of grazing land was called 'right of station'. From that beginning came the sheep stations and cattle stations of today. Which is why the word 'ranch' never got a look-in, and why 'farm' was restricted to properties that grew crops.

In Britain, government employees, especially bureaucrats, are called *civil servants* but in Australia they are *public servant*s. Why the switch? Are they less public in Britain? Less civil in Australia? Well, it turns out that convicts didn't like being called 'convicts' so other terms were coined. Sometimes they were called 'government men' or 'servants of the Crown' but quite commonly (and as early as 1797) they were known as *public servants*.

This term appears to have continued in use into the 1820s, but from as early as 1812 the existing expression was broadened in application to include 'civilian' government employees as well. And from 1852 onwards (the year transportation finally ended) this was the only meaning given to the term. Which is why Australia's civil servants are public servants to this day.

Bushranger – meaning an outlaw living wild and robbing the occasional passers-by – is a distinctively Australian usage of what began as an American term. And it was the convict experience that changed the meaning of the term here.

The *Australian National Dictionary* defines a bushranger as 'one who engages in armed robbery, escaping into, or living in, the bush in the manner of an outlaw'. However, if you check an American dictionary such as the *Merriam-Webster*, the first meaning given for *bushranger* is 'frontiersman; woodsman; one who lives in or frequents a forest: an expert in the arts and skills of living or travelling in the woods; one who works in the woods; *specifically*: a foreman in charge of the felling of trees and removal of logs'. This meaning dates from 1758.

That innocent American meaning appears in Australia quite early in the piece. For instance, the *AND* quotes the following from the papers of Sir Joseph Banks (from 1805): 'If the bush rangers will always bring plants from the remote parts of their tours, I can form a good idea of what distance they have been'.

But the English settlement here was a convict colony, and such an innocent meaning could not long survive. Convicts who didn't fancy working in a road gang in the heat and the humidity took to the bush – officially they 'absconded' or 'bolted'. They then often displayed a remarkable degree of expertise in 'the arts and skills of living or travelling in the woods', to which they added the arts and skills of highway robbery. And so the meaning of the word changed, and the distinctively Aussie notion of a *bushranger* was born. All because of the convict colony.

New chum is a term that for a long time was part of the vernacular of Aussie English. And it hasn't entirely died out. In 1977 Bert Newton referred to himself as 'a *new chum* at Logie presentations'. In other words, a *new chum* was someone who was a novice, who was inexperienced in some field or occupation. Aussie folk songs are filled with references to new chums because for most of the nineteenth century newly arrived immigrants were called new chums.

But it began as a convict term. From the Second Fleet onwards newly arrived prisoners were called *new chums*. That was the source of the term. (And while fellow prisoners were called *chums* in the flash language used by professional criminals in London, the expression *new chum* is only recorded in Australia.)

Muster is another term that began in the convict–military establishment, and then took on a whole new lease of life in the language of rural Australia. *Muster* first appeared in English in the fourteenth century (from an Old French source word) with the meaning of 'to show, display, exhibit'. By the fifteenth century it had taken on a military meaning in the expression *to muster arms* – in other words, to go on parade: to show that you are present and that your arms are in good order.

From this usage came the regular military meaning of *muster*, 'to assemble for inspection'. And that was the meaning that came to these shores with the New South Wales Corps and the convicts they guarded. Not only were the soldiers *mustered* but the same term was applied to the convicts. For instance, John Hunter (Governor Arthur Phillip's second in command and designated successor) could record in his journal in 1789: 'I gave orders for the convicts to be *mustered* in their huts three times every night'. (I'm sure that made him very popular!)

So in the settlement muster came to mean 'a routine assembling of convicts in order to ascertain that all are present'. And even the first census done of the convict colony was called a muster.

By 1813 *muster* had been transferred to life on the land, where it meant 'to gather livestock together for branding, counting or drafting'. To this day *mustering* means 'rounding up livestock' (for shearing or branding or to load them on trucks and ship them off to the abattoirs).

Lexicographer Amanda Laugesen has compiled a dictionary of the language of early colonial Australia called *Convict Words*. She writes that 'The story of the vocabulary of Australian convictism is shaped by the nature of the society it described and from which it emerged'. And she concludes that 'the convict period of Australian history ... contributed a number of colourful and, in some cases, enduring words to Australian English'.

Her book notes that the foundations of Australia produced a unique society in which a new language was created, and she documents the convict words that helped to shape the Australian language – a language that in itself helped to shape a nation.

| | |

All the component parts are now in place: British regional dialect words, the flash language, Aboriginal words and some terms from the convict era. Put them all together in a linguistic melting pot and something new emerges. At first it's not a full-grown language, just a bawling infant. But all the elements are there, and when this infant starts to talk, stands up and begins to walk and then run, there will be no stopping a language as lively as this.

And where would this linguistic baby grow up? Where would it become a strapping youth full of energy and a quite distinctive character? Why – in the bush, of course!

WORD LIST

Below is a small sample of words born in the time of the chain gangs and their guards, but if you want to know more about the language of that time, you should consult Amanda Laugesen's excellent book *Convict Words*.

ABSENTEE a convict who escaped from custody and remained at large.

BAD a term used by convicts to describe another convict who dissociated himself from his fellows and cooperated with police and officials – a *bad fellow*.

BARRACK a building ... for the temporary accommodation of convicts.

BIRTHSTAIN the stigma attached to the convict period or to convict ancestry.

BOLT (of a convict) to escape from custody.

CHAIN GANG a party of convicts assigned to hard labour in chains.

CONVICT-MADE made or constructed by convict labour.

EMANCIPIST a convict who had been pardoned or whose sentence had expired.

EMIGRANT a person who chose to leave their country of origin in order to settle in Australia.

EXCLUSIONIST a person opposed to the integration of ex-convicts into Australian society.

FREE SETTLER an emigrant to Australia who came of his or her free will (i.e. was not transported as a convict).

FREEBOOTER a runaway convict; a bushranger.

GANG a detachment of convicts detailed to public labour.

GENTLEMAN CONVICT a convict with either a liberal education or some training requiring literacy.

GOVERNMENT STROKE a deliberately slow pace of working.

HUT a building for the accommodation of a convict (or convicts).

INCORRIGIBLE a recalcitrant convict.

INDENTURED SERVANT a convict bound over by a contract of service to a private person.

INDULGENCE a mitigation of the conditions under which a convict's sentence was served.

LIFER a person sentenced to transportation to Australia and penal servitude for life.

LOCK-UP a place where a convict was detained if criminal behaviour had been alleged or had occurred.

NIGHT WATCH a party of police, usually selected from among the convicts ('trusties'), who went on patrol during the night hours with authority to secure all persons suspected of committing a crime or intending to do so.

OLD HAND a convict with long experience of life in a penal colony.

OLD LAG a former convict.

OVERSEER a person appointed, frequently from the convict body, to superintend the work of a party of convicts.

PARRAMATTA CLOTH a coarse woollen cloth, originally manufactured by the inmates of the Female Factory (women's prison) at Parramatta.

RATION a fixed allowance of provisions, especially food, provided for convicts.

SLOPS garments and blankets made cheaply from poor material and distributed to convicts.

TICKET OF LEAVE a permit or document that allowed a convict to live and work as a private individual within a stipulated area until the expiration or remission of sentence

VANDEMONIAN a convict who had served a sentence in Tasmania or who had escaped from a prison in Tasmania.

WATCH-HOUSE a building in which suspected lawbreakers were held under temporary arrest.

6

UP THE
BUSH

In 1958 Russel Ward published a book called *The Australian Legend* which persuasively spelt out the impact of the bush on Australian popular culture. And I think it's possible to show that this impact extended to our language.

Basically, what happened very early in the history of the colony is that there were more men than women. Blokes without sheilas have lots of spare energy, so to speak. Energy that has to be burnt up. In this situation they had two choices, either (a) kicking a football around vigorously while shouting a lot at each other or (b) going bush. They chose (b).

For the first twenty-five years the small settlement at Sydney Cove was confined to a relatively narrow coastal strip. Additional settlements had been established at Parramatta, Windsor and elsewhere in the Hawkesbury district, but in the foothills of the Blue Mountains it came to a halt. The steep ravines and deep valleys, thickly covered in tangled scrub, were a seemingly impenetrable barrier. It's not for nothing the Blue Mountains were called the Great Dividing Range.

Then in 1813 a party led by Gregory Blaxland, William Lawson and William Charles Wentworth found a way across the Blue Mountains by avoiding the thick scrub in the valleys and following the more sparsely vegetated ridge-tops.

The colony's surveyor, John Oxley, followed their pioneer path and supervised the building of a track over the mountains. It was, at first, a pretty rough track but it could be travelled on foot or on horseback or by bullock wagons.

In this way the western plains were opened up and those early settlers saw 'the vision splendid of the sunlit plains extended' (in Banjo Paterson's rather nicely chosen words). While farming could be done on the coastal plain, these newly opened broad grazing lands were ideal for sheep and cattle. In fact, any mob of sheep or cattle spotting those rolling grasslands would have recognised them as exactly the sort of all-you-can-eat smorgasbord they'd been hoping for.

In that very early period there were four categories of men who went west to run herds of cattle or flocks of sheep and so open the area that was variously called *the bush* or *the outback* or *the inland*. They were: squatters, convicts, currency lads and old hands.

Squatters were those who settled (or 'squatted') on Crown land to run stock, especially sheep. At first they did so without government permission, but later with a lease or licence –

sometimes paying a mere peppercorn rent. Among the earliest squatters were officers of the New South Wales Corps and other government officials. Later their ranks were boosted by free settlers who had enough capital to buy herds and flocks and move them west. Mind you, among the squatters were quite a number of ex-convicts who'd stolen the herd or flock with which they first stocked their run (and who didn't bother to let the colonial government know where they were or what they were doing).

The *Squatting Act* of 1836 gave every person the right to take up unoccupied land in return for an annual fee of ten pounds ($20) plus a halfpenny (half a cent) for every animal pastured on it. There was no limit to the amount of land that could be 'squatted on' – provided the fees were paid and sufficient stock grazed the land. This meant that those who had already taken up land could now legalise their holding by paying the licence fee.

In this way *squatter* becomes one of the earliest 'bush words' to enter our language. The English word *squatter* came to Australia via America where it was used to mean 'a settler having no formal or legal title to the land occupied by him, especially one occupying land in a district not yet surveyed or apportioned by the government'. It's recorded in the USA with this meaning in 1788 – the same year the British flag was being run up over the convict colony down-under. In 1828 *squatter* is recorded here to mean anyone (but especially an ex-convict) who occupies Crown land without legal title. By 1837 a *squatter* was someone grazing livestock on land having title by either licence or lease.

But by the middle of the nineteenth century *squatter* had

taken on the meaning it still has today: someone with an 'elevated socioeconomic position' because they graze livestock on a large scale.

But although the squatters give us one of our first bush words there were not all that many of them. They were vastly outnumbered by their employees, and these were (for the most part): convicts, currency lads and old hands.

Convicts need no explanation. They were felons still serving their sentence who were assigned to squatters as free labour. They were valued because they were tough. One mid nineteenth-century commentator said 'their bodies seemed to be compounded of iron and leather'. And all they cost was food and lodging.

Currency was the name given in the early nineteenth century to people of European descent born in Australia, especially those with convict parents. They were also sometimes called 'native born'. The nickname came from the fact that, unlike British-born settlers, they were not 'sterling'.

The story behind the use of the word *currency* is that in 1812 Governor Lachlan Macquarie obtained a large supply of Spanish dollars and had a disc punched out of the centre of each. The disc was called a 'dump' with a value of one shilling and three pence (15 cents), and the outer portion was called a 'holey dollar' and was valued at five shillings (50 cents). But this, you see, was just local currency – it wasn't proper British sterling (backed by the Bank of England). In the same way the sons and daughters of convicts were just 'local currency', not proper sterling produced in Britain: hence *currency lads* and *lasses*. So a non-Aboriginal person native to Australia was just local currency.

And it was these sons of convicts (as well as assigned convicts) who became the earliest bush workers on the sprawling grazing properties of the western districts.

They were joined by those known as *old hand*s. These (for the most part) were emancipists – convicts who had been pardoned or whose sentence had expired. At first *old hand* simply meant an experienced convict who'd been in the colony for quite a while, and later the label was applied to immigrants who'd been here for a bit, had some skills, and knew their way around the place. But the term was often used to imply a convict background. In his childhood memoirs, *Illalong Children*, Banjo Paterson remembers knowing shepherds who were *old hands* – meaning ex-convicts.

These, then, were the workers who first settled in the bush (or who tramped around the outback as itinerant workers) and who took with them the infant language that was to grow up into Aussie English: convicts, the sons of convicts, and ex-convicts. Russel Ward makes the point that in 1828 these three groups made up 87 per cent of the European population; and even as late as 1851 they were 59 per cent of the population.

They took with them into the bush English dialect terms, flash words, Aboriginal words and convict terms. On this foundation they built ways of talking about the bush, and working in the bush, that gave Aussie English the distinctive smell of gum leaves it has to this day. Over the decades that followed the bush workers built a language on the foundations already established – a language that often reflected their own characteristics: practical; rough and ready; quick to puncture affectation ('don't have tickets on yourself'); great improvisers; willing to have a go at anything.

That description, by the way, comes from Russel Ward's *The Australian Legend*. He goes on to say that these early bushies wouldn't work hard without a good reason, but they'd knock themselves out in an emergency. They were gamblers and drinkers and inventors of colourful curses. For the most part they were not talkative, inclined to be blokes of few words. However, when they did use words they could be 'the world's best con men' and spin a most persuasive tall tale. They were fiercely independent, sceptical, stoical, and generally opposed to officiousness and authority.

Another side of these bush pioneers was captured by Adam Lindsay Gordon (1833–70) in one of his bush ballads. You'll find these words on his statue in Spring Street, Melbourne:

> Life is mostly froth and bubble,
> > Two things stand like stone:
> Kindness in another's trouble,
> > Courage in your own.

Those words mark the mateship of the bush – the territory that Henry Lawson was later to stake out as his own. But it began in the earliest days of settlement 'further out'. Bush workers in isolated situations in harsh country either looked after each or they died. Taken together those are the characteristics embodied in the language that grew up in the bush.

The early sheep stations where these convicts, sons of convicts and ex-convicts worked were primitive affairs. The permanent dwelling that was called the 'head station' often consisted of little more than a bush hut (perhaps with a verandah on all four sides to keep off some of the heat) and a few sheds and yards.

Beyond that was open grazing land – there were no fences. The job of the shepherd, in those circumstances, was to take a mob of sheep out on the run, find them grass and watch over them, and at night pen them into a rough enclosure made of 'bush fences' (see the Word List below). In this task he might be assisted by his dog. If the shepherd failed to get enough food or (more likely) a balanced diet, he might end up with *Barcoo rot* (the bush name for a common skin infection).

While the authorities (and possibly the squatters) thought of sheep as coming in 'flocks', to the men who worked with the woolly creatures the collective noun for a bunch of sheep was *mob*. *Mob* is recorded in this sense from 1828, although the word is first recorded in English in the late eighteenth century with the meaning of 'crowd or rabble'. Only in the Australian bush was *mob* applied to a herd or flock of animals. The result is that to this day, in Aussie English, *mob* means: a lot; a bunch; *you* can have a *mob of sheep* or a *mob of cattle* or I could talk about *my mob* (meaning my friends) or *your mob* (meaning your friends).

Once a week, or once a fortnight, the shepherd would come back to the head station for his rations (of meat, tea, flour and sugar). Then he'd be off to his lonely life with his mob of sheep again. The head station he came back to (what Americans called the 'ranch house') – however modest it might be – was known in the outback as the *homestead* ('the main residence on a sheep or cattle station or large farm' as the *Macquarie Dictionary* defines it). Although it is a very old English word, this use of the word came to be applied especially to Australia. And only in the Australian bush did a continuous stretch of grazing land come to be called a *run*. The word, of course, has many other uses, but this particular use emerged in Australia and is first recorded in

1804. The development is obvious enough: the grazing land on which you run your sheep or cattle is itself called a *run*.

And then, as the nineteenth century went on, a social demarcation developed in the bush based on the *house*, the *barracks* and the *hut*. The lowest level of hospitality would be offered by the station to an unwashed swaggie who came looking for a handout (possibly a *sundowner* – who arrived at sundown when it was too late in the day to be given a job to do, and who would, therefore, get his handout with no work required). Given his pannikin of flour, he would be told to go and find himself a campsite. So he'd build a small campfire and sleep in the open.

The level up from this gets us onto the bottom of the social ladder. This is the men's *hut*. It was typically a long structure with slab walls and a dirt floor. Double-decker bunks ran around three sides with a fireplace on the fourth. The central table consisted of posts driven into the ground with long slabs laid across them. This is where the station hands would eat and sleep, and any visiting worker (perhaps a bullocky or teamster) would be shown to the hut for his night's accommodation.

The next step up the ladder brings us to the *barracks*. Here there were separate rooms with beds, and the inhabitants were waited on at table by the cook's mate. The people who slept and ate here were the jackaroos (often 'colonial experience men'), the station storekeeper, the overseer, any visiting minor government official and visitors such as cattle-dealers or sheep-buyers.

At the top of the social ladder was the *house* – the main dwelling at the head station. Over the course of the nineteenth century these became larger and grander. Some became two-storey brick buildings with deep verandahs, and multiple bedrooms and reception rooms. This is where the station owner, or his manager, lived along with his family, friends of the family, important visiting government officials, or any other well-connected or important visitors. So grand were some of these buildings that they were sometimes referred to by the men as *government house*. The squatter who rides up on his thoroughbred in 'Waltzing Matilda' probably comes from just such a house.

Meanwhile, the station cook was known either as the *poisoner* or as the *babbling brook* (rhyming slang). If he really could cook, his meals might be described as *bonzer*. This seems to derive (ultimately) from *bon* – the French word for 'good'. It went through a number of variations, including *bonster*, until it settled as *bonzer* (possibly influenced by the Spanish word *bonanza*). Mind you, bonzer didn't become part of Aussie English until quite late in the nineteenth century.

In the second half of the nineteenth century paddocks began to be fenced. Once this happened the *boundary rider* was needed – to check the fences and keep them in order. And once that expression existed it could be borrowed in the twentieth century and applied to footy – to a commentator whose position is at the side of the field rather than in the studio or central commentary position.

Earlier in the nineteenth century the wild horses that thundered through the bush were given the name of *brumbies*. The story goes that a certain Lieutenant Brumby of the New South Wales Corps had imported some good horses while he was still serving in uniform. In 1804 he was transferred to Tasmania, but was unable to muster all his horses before he left – and the horses subsequently ran wild. It's a good story, and may even be true. However, there is an alternative theory that says *brumby* comes from an Aboriginal word, possibly from southern Queensland or northern New South Wales.

Banjo Paterson records the rounding up of such wild horses in 'The Man from Snowy River' and celebrates the mystery surrounding the word in 'Brumby's Run':

> It lies beyond the western pines
> Beneath the sinking sun,
> And not a survey mark defines
> The bounds of 'Brumby's run'.

Pretty much at the bottom of the pecking order among station workers was the *rouseabout*. The word means a general worker, an odd-job man or (sometimes) a casual worker. It's recorded in this sense from 1861. Earlier it had existed as an English dialect word (from Somerset, to be precise) with the meaning of 'a restless, roaming creature'. It seems to come from the verb *to* rouse meaning 'to stir up to movement'. It was used of *rousing* game birds from their nests (so that they could be shot – not that you would have told them that at the time); and *rousing* a sleeping person from their bed. And *rouseabout* was abbreviated (in the common Australian manner) into both *rousie* and *rouser*.

And somewhere along the way a sheep came to be called a *jumbuck*. This is of uncertain origin. It might come from an Aboriginal word (the Kamilaroi language has been suggested), but it seems more likely that it comes from an Aboriginal pidgin version of the English expression 'jump-up' – because jumping up is certainly something sheep do. Wherever it comes from it's important because it's another 'Waltzing Matilda' word. *Jumbuck* is first recorded in 1824.

Meanwhile, back at the homestead the earth-closet toilet (well away from the main buildings, down at the bottom of the home yard) came to be called the *dunny*. The word is recorded in this sense from 1843. *Dunny* seems to have descended from the eighteenth-century British dialect word *dunneken*. The last syllable ('ken') probably comes from a source word meaning 'house', while the first syllable is probably related in some way to 'dung'. Over time *dunny* came to have a wider application, and is now used to name any toilet or lavatory, inside the house as well as out. However, the older, free-standing, outdoor dunny is preserved in some well-known Australian expressions such as 'as lonely as a country dunny' and 'I hope your chooks turn into emus and kick your dunny down'.

Creek is another word that took on a special meaning in the bush. Part of English since the middle of the thirteenth century, *creek* meant 'a narrow inlet in the coastline of the sea, or the tidal estuary of a river'. It was in the bush that *creek* came to mean 'small stream, or the branch of a river.'

|||

At the very end of the nineteenth century CJ Dennis looked back on the pioneering days and celebrated the verbal inventiveness of outback workers in the bush ballad called 'An Old Master'. It's worth quoting in full:

We were cartin' laths and palin's from the slopes of Mount St. Leonard.
With our axles near the road-bed and the mud as stiff as glue;
And our bullocks weren't precisely what you'd call conditioned nicely,
And meself and Messmate Mitchell had our doubts of gettin' through.

It had rained a tidy skyful in the week before we started,
But our tucker-bag depended on the sellin' of our load;
So we punched 'em on by inches, liftin' 'em across the pinches.
Till we struck the final section of the worst part of the road.

We were just congratulatin' one another on the goin',
When we blundered in a pot-hole right within the sight of goal,
Where the bush-track joins the metal. Mitchell, as he saw her settle,
Justified his reputation at the peril of his soul.

We were in a glue-pot certain – red and stiff and most tenacious;
Over naves and over axles – waggon sittin' on the road.
''Struth,' says I, 'they'll never lift her. Take a shot from Hell to shift her.
Nothin' left us but unyoke 'em and sling off the blessed load.'

Now, beside our scene of trouble stood a little one-roomed humpy,
Home of an enfeebled party by the name of Dad McGee.
Daddy was, I pause to mention, livin' on an old age pension
Since he gave up bullock punchin' at the age of eighty-three.

Startled by our exclamations, Daddy hobbled from the shanty.
Gazin' where the stranded wagon looked like some half-foundered ship.
When the state o' things he spotted, 'Looks,' he said, 'like you was
    potted',
And he toddles up to Mitchell. 'Here,' says he, 'gimme that whip.'

Well! I've heard of transformations; heard of fellers sort of changin'
In the face of sudden danger or some great emergency;
Heard the like in song and story and in bush traditions hoary,
But I nearly dropped me bundle as I looked at Dad McGee.

While we gazed he seemed to toughen; as his fingers gripped the handle
His old form grew straight and supple, and a light leapt in his eye;
And he stepped around the wagon, not with footsteps weak and laggin',
But with firm, determined bearin', as he flung the whip on high.

Now he swung the leaders over, while the whip-lash snarled and volleyed;
And they answered like one bullock, strainin' to each crack and clout;
But he kept his cursin' under till old Brindle made a blunder;
Then I thought all Hell had hit me, *and the master opened out.*

And the language! Oh, the language! Seemed to me I must be dreamin';
While the wondrous words and phrases only genius could produce
Roared and rumbled, fast and faster, in the throat of that Old Master –
Oaths and curses tipped with lightning, cracklin' flames of fierce abuse.

Then we knew the man before us was a Master of our callin';
One of those great lords of language gone forever from Out-back;
Heroes of an ancient order; men who punched across the border;
Vanished giants of the sixties; puncher-princes of the track.

Now we heard the timbers strainin', heard the waggon's loud
    complainin',
And the master cried triumphant, as he swung 'em into line,
As they put their shoulders to it, lifted her, and pulled her through it:
'That's the way we useter to do it in the days o' sixty-nine!'

Near the foot of Mount St. Leonard lives an old, enfeebled party
Who retired from bullock-punchin' at the age of eighty-three.
If you seek him folk will mention, merely, that he draws the pension;
But to us he looms a Master – Prince of Punchers, Dad McGee!

It would be possible to fill not just a chapter but a whole book with the verbal invention that went on in those years in the Australian bush.

So, what was happening, exactly, and why? My suggestion is that those early bush workers (convicts, the sons of convicts and ex-convicts) took with them not just the verbal ingredients – English dialect terms, flash words, Aboriginal words and convict terms – but an awareness of language and an interest in language.

Those four ingredients, I suggest, not only supplied the foundation, and some of the raw materials, but stimulated the whole process. They made those first bush workers (and the ones who came after them) especially aware of language. They caused those bush workers, sitting around in the men's hut at night, to take delight in finding new applications for old words, and in coining new expressions.

For this reason it was in the bush that the infant form of Aussie English grew up. By the middle of the nineteenth century Aussie English was a vigorous and healthy young adult, with a distinctive character, ready for its next major kick-along – the discovery of gold.

WORD LIST

Now, I'm sure there can be no one who doubts the impact of the bush on the development of Aussie English, but just to drive the point home: in the *Australian National Dictionary* there are twelve pages of entries incorporating the word 'bush'. That's thirty-six columns! Below is a small selection from that list (just some of the words and their meanings – if you want to see the citations they're based on you'll have to go to the *AND*).

BUSH (1) natural vegetation; (2) country which remains in its natural state; (3) the country as opposed to the town (from the Dutch word *bosch*, 'woodland').

BUSH BALLAD a poem in a ballad metre about life in the bush (especially the verse of Banjo Paterson, Henry Lawson and other poets of *The Bulletin*).

BUSH BAPTIST person of vague but strong religious beliefs.

BUSH BED a bed made at a campsite from light branches and long grass.

BUSH BISCUIT a thin cake of flour and water baked on the hot embers of a campfire.

BUSH BLOW clearing one's nose without the use of a handkerchief.

BUSH BREAD damper, made from a simple flour and water dough, cooked in the coals or in a camp oven.

BUSH BROTHERHOOD an Anglican missionary organisation founded to provide an itinerant ministry in remote areas.

BUSH CARPENTER a rough amateur carpenter.

BUSH CHOOK (1) emu; (2) Tasmanian native hen.

BUSH CONSTABLE an ex-convict, or ticket-of-leave man, or a local Aboriginal man, sworn in as a constable to help maintain law and order.

BUSH COOK a rough-and-ready cook of limited skill (the nickname for such cooks was 'poisoners' – which will give you some idea of their skills).

BUSH FASHION an indifferent, slapdash style; something thrown together any-old-how has been put together *bush fashion.*

BUSH FEED a big meal; can refer to abundant feed for stock or the size of meal a hungry stockman can knock over.

BUSH FENCE a rough enclosure for animals made by piling up cut scrub.

BUSH FEVER a longing to return to the bush.

BUSH FOAL a child born out of wedlock.

BUSH HONEY honey from the nests of native bees.

BUSH HOSPITALITY generous, open-handed hospitality.

BUSH HUT very modest accommodation; often (in the early years) nothing more than slab walls, dirt floor and bark roof.

BUSH KNIFE a large knife with many uses (the sort of impressive blade flashed by Crocodile Dundee on the streets of New York).

BUSH LAWYER (1) an argumentative person, especially one who attempts complicated and often specious arguments to prove a point; (2) a person who pretends to a knowledge of the law.

BUSH MADNESS a common affliction in the early years, caused by living alone with only sheep and kangaroos to talk to (when they start talking back you have *bush madness*).

BUSH MILE longer than a mile in town ... or, at least, it feels that way.

BUSH MISSIONARY one who, in the early years, travelled up the country to teach the Bible to shepherds and other remote bush workers.

BUSH PARSON a minister who builds a church and cares for a congregation in a remote area.

BUSH POET the writers of bush ballads and their modern imitators.

BUSH RACES an informal race meeting, organised by the local community, and held in a paddock (often a paddock not too far from a pub).

BUSH ROAD one where the bushes have been cleared, banks of rivers and gullies levelled, trees notched on the route, and cuts made on the tops or faces of hills where necessary, the remainder being left in a natural state.

BUSH SCHOOL a one-room, one-teacher school located in the back-blocks.

BUSH SHOWER a tin with holes punched in the bottom hanging from a gum tree, under which it is possible to shower as the water runs out.

BUSH TEA strong, black tea boiled in a billy over a camp fire and sweetened with coarse, dark sugar.

BUSH TELEGRAPH gossip; information passed on from person to person.

BUSH TUCKER (1) simple fare, as eaten by one living in or off the bush; (2) food from Australian indigenous plants and trees.

BUSH WEEK a fictitious festival when *bushies* come to town; the expression is used ironically by someone who suspects they are being made the victim of a scam or prank, as in the question 'What do you think this is, bush week?' To which the proper response is, 'Yes, and you're the sap!'

BUSH YARD stakes of wood driven into the ground with tree branches in between, used as a temporary holding yard for animals.

BUSHED lost in the bush; or just lost, in a general sense (either literally or metaphorically).

BUSHFIRE a wildfire that burns out of control through bushland (often threatening farmland, buildings, towns or suburbs).

BUSHMAN someone skilled in living, working and travelling in the bush.

BUSHY (also *bushie*) countrified; lacking the supposed refinements of urban life.

TAKE TO THE BUSH to run away; to escape from custody (originally of convicts); to leave the town for the country.

TO GO BUSH to escape; to disappear from one's usual haunts; to leave the beaten track and travel cross-country; to leave the urban life for that of the country.

7

GOLD!

Today if you long to see the mass movement of vast numbers of people you need to linger in the general vicinity of the MCG on Grand Final day. But in the mid nineteenth century what moved the masses to flock to a place in large numbers was not football, but gold.

It began with the Californian gold rush of 1849. A significant number of blokes from the Colony of New South Wales (which at that time covered the whole of eastern Australia) hopped ship and sailed across the Pacific to try their luck.

One of them was a cove named Edward Hammond Hargraves. In fact, he had little luck on the Californian goldfields, and a year later he was back down-under. But he had brought back with him some knowledge of how to pan for gold. Hargraves taught the little he knew to John Lister and the brothers William and James Tom. In fact, it was Lister and the Tom brothers who found payable gold, but it was Hargraves who drummed up all the publicity and received the official rewards.

Hargraves himself found a few specks of gold in the Bathurst district in February 1851, but it was Lister and the Toms who had a major find in April of that same year on the Turon River. On that basis of that major find – and Hargraves' flair for publicity – the gold rushes came to Australia.

It was in Victoria (which had become a separate colony in 1851) that the biggest and most spectacular finds were made: Ballarat, Bendigo and half a dozen other places became major goldfields. A third of the world's gold output between 1851 and 1861 came from Victoria. The entire population of the continent was seized with gold fever – producing that wild gleam in the eye seen nowadays only in the eye of someone keen to lose weight and has discovered a new diet. In New South Wales there were active goldfields at Ophir, Turon, Hill End and elsewhere.

Queensland became a separate colony in 1859 – and by the 1860s gold was being found there too, and many of the diggers were rushing north. Queensland's biggest gold rush was at Palmer River, beginning in 1874.

Then the focus shifted westward to the Colony of Western Australia (which had been founded in 1829). There was a major gold find at Coolgardie in 1892, followed a year later by Hannan's Rush – named after Paddy Hannan. In 1895 this spot on the map was renamed Kalgoorlie.

What all these gold rushes were about was people – vast numbers of people. They had the effect of raising the population of Australia from less than half a million in 1851 to more than three times that number just twenty years later. And the newcomers flocked here from around the world.

There were Americans (looking for richer pickings than on the Californian fields); Irish; Scots; English toffs with Oxbridge accents; working class Englishmen from the shires; French; Germans; Italians; New Zealanders; and large numbers of Chinese. In fact, racial intolerance and fears of economic competition combined to cause a number of anti-Chinese riots.

What this vast inrush of immigrants did was to make the distinctiveness of Aussie English stand out. Where a visiting Yank might have said, 'You guys sure have a funny way of talking', the Oxford graduate (a bit further down the stream, panning for gold) might have remarked, 'You chappies have a decidedly odd way of expressing yourselves'.

The multitudinous visitors with their many voices and accents made the mature, and now vigorous, Aussie English stand out as a distinctive and colourful dialect – a bright new contribution to the world family of the English language.

Dr Bruce Moore has edited a glossary of the language of the nineteenth-century Australian gold rushes called *Gold! Gold! Gold!* In the introduction he writes: 'The contribution of the gold rushes to Australian English lies not so much in the individual lexical items, but in the impetus it gave to the separate identity of Australian English.'

We have already told the story of the elements that gave rise to Aussie English, and of how this infant language grew up in the bush. And it all happened very quickly. As early as 1828 (just forty years after the first settlement) there are references to a 'colonial language'. A newspaper advertisement by an English gentleman that appeared in a Hobart paper, the *Tasmanian*, on 15 August 1828, said: 'If you know of any person who is proficient in the Colonial language, you will do me a great service by recommending them to me, as I am resolved that my children shall not remain ignorant of the dialect of the land they live in.' And if you think you detect a hint of a sneer in such expressions as 'colonial language', 'colonial parlance' and 'colonial phrases' you're not too wide of the mark.

What the gold rushes did – with their vast influx of foreigners – was to make the distinctiveness of this vigorous new language even more obvious. Of course, it was not yet called Aussie English – but that's what it was, and it was quite capable of knocking the wind out of snobby visitors.

In 1854 Catherine Helen Spence published a novel called *Clara Morrison*, subtitled *A Tale of South Australia During the Gold Fever*. In it she captures exactly the astonishment provoked by Aussie English:

> 'He does not come up to your mark by a long chalk,'
> laughed Minnie.
>
> 'What *did* you say?' exclaimed Miss Withering, in a tone of utter amazement.
>
> 'I meant that he has not nearly eighteen hundred a year,' said Minnie, blushing at having been led into speaking colonial slang.
>
> 'Oh! Is that what you meant? I understand *English*, but I see you colonists are corrupting the language sadly …'

It's interesting to reflect that in the twenty-first century we find it hard to believe that anyone could be astonished by such an expression as 'He does not come up to your mark by a long chalk' – but that's because we are totally immersed in Aussie English, and its phrases and constructions sound perfectly normal to us.

Bruce Moore makes the comment that 'one of the effects of the gold rushes was to exacerbate the conflict between sterling (those born in the United Kingdom) and currency (those born in Australia) that had begun in the early days of the colony. This was a social conflict that was to develop into a linguistic conflict.'

This vigorous young language (or, more precisely, this new dialect of the English language) that had grown up in the Aussie bush now stood out as something glaringly new and different, which is why Bruce Moore writes: 'The gold-rush period – with its massive increase in population, and its dissemination (especially through the popular press) of gold terminology and other elements of the lexicon of "colonial jingo" – played a significant role in the creation of Australian English.' And (as we'll see in chapter 17) the gold rushes also played a role in the development of the Australian accent.

But let's take a couple of examples from the vigorous young language, beginning with that most Aussie of all words: *digger*. One of the definitions the *Macquarie Dictionary* offers for *digger* is 'cobber, or mate'. In other words, it is one of those words that pulsates at the heart of Australia's popular culture – as part of what Russel Ward calls 'the Australian legend.'

Digger has this power because of its use by Australian soldiers in the First World War – by those who forged the legend of the Anzacs in the heat of combat. WH Dowling's book of Aussie slang from World War I is called *Digger Dialect*s, and he defines *digger* as 'an Australian soldier (strictly an infantryman).' (The name of Dowling's book alone is significant. And when Amanda Laugesen compiled a glossary of the language used by Australians at war she called her book *Diggerspeak*. We'll meet both these books again – in chapters 11 and 13 respectively.)

But although that's where the word's emotive power comes from, *digger* was not born in the beaches of Gallipoli – but on the goldfields. The history of the word runs like this: It (obviously) begins with the verb 'to dig', and that goes all the way back to Norman French *digeur*, brought to England by William and his conquering army. Out of this verb the noun *digger* (with the obvious meaning of 'one who digs') emerged in the fifteenth century. And it remained a menial word for agricultural workers or miners until the nineteenth century, when it was given a new lease of life as the special word to label someone working on the Australian goldfields. One of the definitions of *digger* in the *Oxford English Dictionary* is 'one who digs or searches for gold in a goldfield' – and the earliest citation given to support this meaning is from Australia.

The *Australian National Dictionary* has managed to turn up an Australian citation from as early as 1849. Then (the *AND* explains) this word was transferred (during the wars of 1914–18 and 1939–45) to 'a (private) soldier from Australia or New Zealand'. Then (the same authoritative source continues), *digger* was 'increasingly [restricted to] an Australian soldier exclusively'.

The next stage in its development was its use in civilian as well as military contexts as a term of address 'frequently [explains the *AND*] shortened to *Dig*'. In other words, it became one of those handy words one Aussie male could use in speaking to another he hadn't seen for some time and whose name he had forgotten: 'G'day mate!' would cover the situation, but 'G'day digger!' worked just as well.

And it all began on the Australian goldfields. Perhaps it's worth asking why. One suggestion is that the word was transferred to soldiers because of the trenches they had to dig. However, it seems to me more likely that the battlefield re-created the situation of mutual dependence that existed on the goldfields (and in the bush). And that sense of depending on your friends for your survival is what's captured by words such as 'mate' and 'digger'.

That's why *digger* covers almost exactly the same range of ideas and feelings that Henry Lawson refers to as 'mateship'.

Once *digger* had taken on its special meaning, it bred a whole glossary of words:

> **digger costume** the characteristic attire of the digger
> consisting of a blue shirt (or, less commonly, a red shirt)
> with bush boots and moleskin trousers.
>
> **diggerdom** referring to diggers as a social group, or a force;
> the digging class.
>
> **diggeress** (now long-forgotten, fortunately) the wife or female
> companion of a digger.
>
> **digger hunt** a raid made by the police on a goldfield for the
> purpose of hunting down diggers lacking a gold licence.

And there were self-explanatory expressions such as 'digger's bride' and 'digger's wedding'. The former was (apparently) the goal of many a colonial girl, and the latter was a lavish affair, with the wedding party parading in carriages through the streets of a major city.

And the goldfields also gave us another distinctly Aussie word in *fossick*. When some episodes of the British television series *Antiques Roadshow* were filmed on location in Australia one of the local guests said, 'Here's something I found *fossicking* in the junk room'. The visiting English expert looked puzzled. After some explanation the visitor said, 'Ah, yes, you mean *rummaging*'.

We can easily forget that *fossicking* is an Australian word. The verb *to fossick* is first recorded from 1852, in the *Australian Gold Diggers' Monthly Magazine*. And that's where it came from – the goldfields. Originally it meant 'searching for gold on the surface, especially in a careless and unsystematic way'. Nowadays we can *fossick around* for anything, but originally you fossicked by looking for surface gold in loose dirt around the diggings.

Fossick seems to be another of those dialect words that died out back in the UK while surviving here. A *fossicker* may have originally been a troublesome person (according to the *Oxford English Dictionary*). And at the diggings someone who came along to potter around your dirt heaps to pick up what you missed would certainly be looked upon as troublesome.

Nowadays *fossick* is a mild and harmless term. The *Macquarie Dictionary* says that it means 'to search for small items'.

And this is as good a place as any to explore the origins of the expression *kangaroo court*. The *Macquarie Dictionary* defines a *kangaroo court* as 'an unauthorised or irregular court conducted with disregard for or perversion of legal procedure, as a mock court by prisoners in a jail, or by trade unionists in judging workers who do not follow union decisions'.

It should be an Aussie expression – but it's not. And it should come from the Aussie goldfields – but it doesn't. In fact, *kangaroo court* appears to have arisen in the United States. The earliest citation is from Texas in the second half of the nineteenth century. The suggestion has been made that the term was born on the goldfields of California.

The phrase may have been coined because, as already noted, there were Australians who'd joined the rush, and were teaching the Yanks a word or two. Or it may be that the first such rough-justice tribunals were aimed at punishing claim jumpers – and anyone who's a 'jumper' can be nicknamed a 'kangaroo'. So (perhaps) originally the expression may have referred to the accused, rather than the fact that the so-called court leapt to judgment in a single bound (with the agility of an Australian macropod).

The connection between *kangaroo court* and the Aussie goldfields may be remote – but it may be there, in the form of the Aussies who went to California and brought their gold hunting skills back home when the gold rushes began here.

But leaving that linguistic oddity to one side, the real role of the gold rushes in the development of Aussie English was that the massive migration sparked by the discovery of gold compelled the local population to face the fact that they were speaking their own dialect. British linguistic snobbery towards Australia (and the cultural cringe some Australians felt in consequence) began with this discovery.

By the time gold had tripled the population of Australia, everyone knew that a new dialect had developed on this continent – one that was rich, colourful and inventive; one that had a vocabulary and a sound that was all its own.

WORD LIST

Below is a sampling of the language of the nineteenth-century Australian gold rushes. If you'd like to know more, the book you'll need to consult is *Gold! Gold! Gold!* (2000) edited by Bruce Moore.

BAIL OUT emptying water from a flooded hole or shaft.

BANDICOOT, TO another word for *fossicking*, especially in the sense of working over previously worked ground, in the hope of discovering particles of gold missed by earlier diggers. *To bandicoot* remains a regional expression in some parts of Australia with the meaning of 'to steal potatoes from a field or garden by digging under the plant without disturbing its top'. (It can be used of other fruit and veg obtained in a similarly secretive fashion.)

BARK HUT a digger's temporary dwelling constructed from bark. Such dwellings were common on the goldfields. Later in the nineteenth century (as the big squatting properties were broken up) pioneer selectors often lived in a bark hut until they could build something more permanent. This sort of dwelling was commemorated in the Aussie folk song 'The Old Bark Hut'.

BLACK TROOPER an Aboriginal man recruited to be a trooper on the diggings.

BLANK an unproductive mine (probably related to the familiar expression 'to draw a blank' – which comes from the notion of a drawing a blank lottery ticket: one that wins no money).

BLOCK OFF to place markers at the angles of a mining claim, as required by law. From this, probably, comes the distinctively Australian expressions 'block of land' or 'house block', meaning a piece of land large enough to a build a family home on. Elsewhere 'block' (when referring to land) usually means an entire neighbourhood – the area surrounded on four sides by streets.

BLUE SHIRT the distinguishing garment worn by the digger. It became his emblem or badge in the same sense that the blue collar was the emblem of the manual worker and the white collar the emblem of the office worker. In just that way a labourer on the goldfields could be called a *blue shirt*.

DART wash dirt (from which alluvial gold was extracted). *Dart* was a British dialect pronunciation of 'dirt'; it's the same pronunciation that gave us the term 'the Old Dart' for England.

DIGGINGS, THE always used in the plural, and meaning the goldfields.

DRAY a two-wheeled cart, commonly used by diggers travelling to and from the diggings. It became a common bush vehicle, and inspired the Aussie folk song 'The Old Bullock Dray'.

DRY BLOWER an apparatus used in 'dry blowing', in which a current of air was used to separate particles of gold from the dirt or sand in which it was found. Common on the Western Australian goldfields where water was scarce. I've included the term here because one of Australia's leading bush balladists, EG Murphy, wrote under the penname of 'Dryblower'.

DUFFER an unproductive shaft or hole producing little or no gold.

ESCORT armed troopers responsible for protecting gold being shipped from the diggings to a city bank.

EUREKA the name given to a large deposit of alluvial gold found near Ballarat early in 1852. When diggers clashed with the police and military over the unfair gold licensing system in 1854, the site of that find was where the Eureka Stockade was erected and where the Eureka flag (the Southern Cross, in white against a blue background) was first flown. The issue was the same one that triggered off the American Revolution: 'no taxation without representation'. The vast majority of diggers had no vote in choosing the colonial government, and yet that government imposed a burdensome tax in the form of the monthly gold licence. The battle at the stockade was over in a matter of hours, when troopers stormed the hastily built walls in darkness while the diggers slept. But (in the end) most of the diggers' demands were granted.

GOLDEN MILE a rich area between Kalgoorlie and Boulder in Western Australia.

GOLD! GOLD! GOLD! Nowadays we are most likely to associate this with Norman May's famous call of the swimming at the 1980 Moscow Olympics. What Norman really said on that occasion was: 'Gold! Gold! Gold for Australia!' But the three words (with the exclamation marks) were common in the newspapers of the mid nineteenth century as goldfields were discovered one after another.

GROG SHOP / GROG SHANTY *grog* was British slang for alcohol (especially rum). Rough unlicensed pubs on the early goldfields were called *grog shop*s or *grog shanties*. The first of those two expressions has never quite gone away, and to this day an Aussie will sometimes call a pub or a bottle shop a *grog shop*.

HUMP to hoist or carry on the back; later, itinerant bush workers talked about 'humping a swag' around the bush.

JOE a mocking nickname for the police or troopers who carried out digger hunts, requiring diggers to produce their gold licence; it probably comes from the name of the Lieutenant-Governor of Victoria during the 1851–54 period, Charles Joseph La Trobe (nicknamed 'Charley Joe').

JUGULAR a vein of gold (a joking comparison with the human jugular vein).

MOLESKIN TROUSERS moleskin was a tough cotton, the surface of which had been shaved before being dyed, with the result that it resembled the skin of a mole; trousers made from this material became common among workers in the bush and on the diggings.

MULLOCK mining refuse; it came originally from an English dialect word, and survived here, especially in the form of *mullocky*, meaning 'rubbishy' or 'messy' (a term Aussie mums have used to describe their kids' rooms from time to time).

PAN OUT / PAN OFF to search for particles of gold by washing alluvial, gold-bearing deposits to separate out the gold. If you find gold then things 'pan out well'; if there's no colour in the bottom of the pan at the end of the wash then things 'haven't panned out well'.

ROARING DAYS, THE the time of the gold rushes; a favourite expression of Henry Lawson.

STROKE work, as in such expressions as 'to do a fair stroke' or 'he wouldn't do a stroke'.

TINNED DOG canned meat; this term is especially associated with the Western Australian goldfields where there was a shortage of fresh meat.

TRAP police officer or trooper.

YELLOW FEVER a lust or craze for finding gold; Australia was gripped by *yellow fever* in the 1850s.

8

AUSTRAL ENGLISH

The gold rushes have brought us up to the 1850s and 60s. We now leap ahead to 1898. In that year a book called *A Dictionary of Austral English* was published – the first formal and scholarly dictionary of the new dialect I'm calling Aussie English. But we haven't missed out on the intervening years, because *Austral English* is a book that looks back and collects the words and expressions that had come to typify Aussie English from the time European settlement of the great south land began.

The story of Austral English begins not here but in England in the year 1857. In that year Richard Chevenix Trench read a paper to the Philological Society of London entitled 'On Some

Deficiencies in our English Dictionaries'. This led the society to launch a project that aimed to collect enough materials to publish something they intended to call the *New English Dictionary on Historical Principles*.

Instead of taking a few years and filling four volumes this project ended up taking sixty-nine years and filling twelve volumes – over 15 000 pages reporting on more than 400 000 words. It is known today as the *Oxford English Dictionary*.

The first two editors (Herbert Coleridge and Frederick Furnivall) got the work started and took it up to 1879. But it was the third editor, appointed in that year, who really shaped the massive work. Named Dr James H Murray, he set up an orderly system for collecting citations, arranging material, writing definitions and etymologies (that's the sources of words) and publishing the unwieldy thing bit by bit, as the work was done.

One of the main contributions Murray made was to invite readers around Britain, and around the world, to contribute what lexicographers call 'citations'. A citation is a passage (a quotation) from a publication that shows how a word has been used. Because Murray wanted to trace the history and the development of the meaning of each of those 400 000 words he needed citations from their earliest use to the present day. That meant reading books, newspapers, magazines – just about anything written in English, from the birth of the English language up until the nineteenth century.

That task was far beyond Murray and his small team, hence his brilliant stroke of using newspapers to invite readers from around the world to contribute citations. Murray ended up with readers all over Britain and the United States poring over the publications that he wanted checked, copying out citations and posting them to him.

Which brings us to the author of *A Dictionary of Austral English*.

His name was Edward Ellis Morris (1843–1902). He was born in Madras, India, in the days when India was under British rule. He was educated in Britain (at Rugby and Oxford) and came to the Colony of Victoria in 1875 to take up the post of headmaster of the Melbourne Church of England Grammar School. In 1882 Morris became Professor of English at the University of Adelaide, and two years later Professor of Modern Languages and Literature at the University of Melbourne.

Perhaps more importantly, he settled in and made this place his home. He married a local girl, and his children (three girls and a boy) were all born here. He became a prominent Melburnian – active and influential in the Church of England, in the management of Melbourne Public Library, and in charitable organisations (as well as the university). And as someone born and educated overseas his ear was well tuned to pick up the 'colonial dialect' that was spoken here.

When Dr James Murray beavering away at his massive dictionary in Oxford invited contributions from that far-distant corner of the British Empire known as 'Australasia', it was Edward Morris who responded to the call. Morris began to collect citations from Australian books, newspapers and magazines and posted them off to Murray. Morris's contributions to the *Oxford English Dictionary* were significant – both in quality and number. However, he realised that there was something else that he could do with his mountain of citations.

Let Dr Morris himself take up the story in his own words:

Instances of words must be noted as one comes across them, and of course they do not in occur in alphabetical order. The work took time, and when my parcel of quotations had grown into a considerable heap, it occurred to me that the collection, if a little further trouble were expended upon it, might first enjoy an independent existence. Various friends kindly contributed more quotations: and this Book is the result.

The 'Book' was published by Macmillan & Company in London in 1898. It was regarded as such a significant achievement that it prompted the University of Melbourne to award Morris the degree of Doctor of Letters.

It was called *A Dictionary of Austral English*, using 'austral' to mean 'southern' – because as well as covering the Australian colonies the dictionary included words from New Zealand. And in his introduction Morris made the same point that I've made in chapter 1 – namely, that our dialect (Aussie English) includes a lot more than just slang words. For instance, Morris included a great deal of natural history in his dictionary – local names for local flora and fauna.

In his introduction Morris cites two sources of new words in particular. The first is what he called 'altered English' – using a common English word in a different way. For instance, the Australian bird that early settlers called a 'magpie' is completely unrelated to the common European bird of that name. The European bird belongs to the species *Pica caudata*, while the scientific name for what we call a magpie in Australia is *Cracticus tibicen*. But a name was needed for the local black and white bird with the large bill, so the English name was borrowed and used (in an 'altered way').

Morris's second main source of new words was the Aboriginal languages. He writes: 'Many of the new Australasian words are taken from the languages of the aborigines, often with considerable alteration due to misunderstanding'.

What is really significant about all this is that a dictionary of over 500 pages could be published around 120 years after English settlement of this continent. In that (historically) short period of time a distinctive dialect had developed (beginning with four sources: the English dialect words, the flash language, convict terms and Aboriginal words). It had rapidly grown into an inventive language full of new coinages. Just how different it was the gold rushes (with their massive intake of migrants) had made obvious to everyone.

And now this dialect (this 'Aussie English') had its first scholarly dictionary, produced on the same historical principles that were guiding the production of the great *Oxford English Dictionary*, with each entry supported by carefully selected quotations.

By my estimate Morris's 500 pages contain around 2000 headwords – each with its definition (and he was a dab hand at writing definitions) supported by the evidence of a list of quotations (in some cases, quite a long list). As an example, here's Morris's complete entry on the slang expression *duck-shoving*:

> **duck-shoving** and **duck-shover**, *n.* a cabman's phrase. In Melbourne, before the days of trams, the wagonette-cabs used to run from fixed stations at so much (generally threepence) a passenger. A cabman who did not wait his turn on the station rank, but touted for passengers up and down the street in the neighbourhood of the rank, was termed a *Duck-shover*.
>
> 1870. D. Blair, 'Notes and Queries,' Aug. 6, p. 111:

'Duck-shoving is the term used by our Melbourne cabmen
to express the unprofessional trick of breaking the rank, in
order to push past the cabman on the stand for the purpose of
picking up a stray passenger or so.'

1896. 'Otago Daily Times,' Jan. 25, p. 3, col. 6:
'The case was one of series of cases of what was technically
known as "duck shoving," a process of getting passengers
which operated unfairly against the cabmen who stayed on the
licensed stand and obeyed the by-law.'

Today we might use *duck-shoving* to describe a politician who
is pushing himself for an appointment ahead of more senior
colleagues, or a sportsman who is angling for selection to a
team despite relative lack of experience. And these usages have
grown out of this Melbourne cabbies' expression from the late
nineteenth century.

Sometimes Morris's treatment of a word was exhaustive. For
instance, his entry on *kangaroo* runs to seven pages!

He was, as you can see, a serious and scholarly dictionary
maker. To give you more of the flavour of Austral English here
is one of his natural history entries. This one deals with the
Bogong moth and is reproduced in full:

> **bugong**, or **bogong**, or **bougong**, *n*. an Australian moth,
> *Danais limniace*, or *Agrotis spina*, eaten by the aborigines.
> 1834. Rev. W. B. Clarke, 'Researches in the Southern Gold
> Fields of New South Wales' (second edition), p. 228:

'These moths have obtained their name from their occurrence on the "Bogongs" or granite mountains. They were described by my friend Dr. Bennett in his interesting work on "New South Wales," 1832–4, as abundant on the Bogong Mountain, Tumut River. I found them equally abundant, and in full vigour, in December, coming in clouds from the granite peaks of the Muniong Range. The blacks throw them on the fire and eat them.'

1859. H. Kingsley, 'Geoffrey Hamlyn,' p. 355:
'The westward range is called the Bougongs. The blacks during summer are in the habit of coming thus far to collect and feed on the great grey moths (bougongs) which are found on the rocks.'

1871. 'The Athenæum,' May 27, p. 660:
'The Gibbs Land and Murray districts have been divided into the following counties: ... Bogong (native name of grubs and moths).'

1878. R. Brough Smyth, 'The Aborigines of Victoria,' Vol. i, p. 207:
'The moths – the Bugong moths – (*Agrotis suffusa*) are greedily devoured by the natives; and in former times, when they were in season, they assembled in great numbers to eat and they grew fat on this food.' [Also a long footnote.]

1890. Richard Helms, 'Records of the Australian Museum,' Vol. i, No. 1:
'My aim was to obtain some "Boogongs," the native name for

the moths which so abundantly occur on this range, and no doubt have given it its name.'

1896. 'Sydney Mail,' April 4, Answers to Correspondents: 'It cannot be stated positively, but it is thought that the name of the moth "bogong" is taken from that of the mountain. The meaning of the word is not known, but probably it is an aboriginal word.'

Three of those quotations are from books, two are from journals, and one is from a newspaper. They are arranged chronologically from the earliest to the latest. This is dictionary making on the historical principles of Dr James Murray of *Oxford English Dictionary* fame – and it is remarkable that it was being done in Australia even before the first edition of the *OED* was complete.

This historical method shows the development of the word, the various spellings, the uncertainty as to whether the moth was named for the mountain, or the mountain for the moth, and records, as well, the attitudes of the times.

Professor Morris was not without his critics. For a start, he was a city man and not a bushman. Secondly, despite his long years here he remained, at heart, an English gentleman. And thirdly, he thought and wrote like a professor of language and literature – rather than like an ordinary Aussie. And those factors gave his book (monumental achievement though it was) certain weaknesses.

For instance, *The Bulletin* refused to be impressed: 'Professor Morris seems hampered by uneasy gentility', it wrote, adding that it seemed odd to imagine someone 'sitting down to compile an Australian slang dictionary with kid gloves on his hands, wadding in his ears, and blushes flooding his manly cheeks'.

And although Morris was setting out to do far more than just record Aussie slang (he was trying to capture a much wider cross-section of our distinctive dialect), there is some truth in *The Bulletin*'s criticism. In his introduction to the second impression Professor HL Rogers writes: 'It must be admitted that *Austral English* is far from being a complete or wholly accurate record of colloquial Australian'.

At the same time, Morris's book was the most substantial attempt to record Aussie English until the Second World War – when Sidney J Baker began work on his landmark book *The Australian Language*.

Morris's book was also limited (as was James Murray's great work) by its reliance on written citations (with the result that the spoken language slipped under the radar). Nevertheless, *A Dictionary of Austral English* was the first scholarly recognition that a new a distinctive dialect had grown up in the great south land. It was the scholarly evidence (if such evidence was needed) that we had our very own language – and in the fervently nationalistic atmosphere of the 1890s it was a language that was gleefully acknowledged and joyfully celebrated in the colonies that were about to become a nation.

In fact, the creative flexibility and sheer verbal vigour of this language was something that *The Bulletin* (the 'bushman's bible'), and its star bush-balladist, Banjo Paterson, were about to demonstrate.

WORD LIST

Below are some sample entries from *Austral English*. I have omitted most of Morris's citations, but his word choices and his definitions give the flavour of his book. (All the definitions are in Morris's own words.)

__ABSENTEE__ a euphemistic term for a convict.

__ASSIGNEE__ a convict assigned as a servant.

__AUSTRALIA__ As early as the sixteenth century there was a belief in a *Terra Australis* ... literally 'southern land,' which was believed to be land lying round and stretching outwards from the South Pole ... The name *Australia* was adapted from the Latin name *Terra Australis*. The earliest suggestion of the word is credited to [Matthew] Flinders, who certainly thought he was inventing the name. (See quotation 1814.) Twenty-one years earlier, however, the word is found (see quotation 1793); and the passage containing it is the first known use of the word in print ...

1793. G. Shaw and J. E. Smith, 'Zoology and Botany of New Holland,' p. 2:
'The vast Island or rather Continent of Australia, Australasia, or New Holland, which has so lately attracted the particular attention of European navigators and naturalists, seems to abound in scenes of peculiar wildness and sterility.'

1814. M. Flinders, 'Voyage to Terra Australis,' Introduction, p. iii, and footnote:
'I have ... ventured upon the re-adoption of the original *Terra Australis*, and of this term I shall hereafter make use, when

speaking of New Holland [the West] and New South Wales, in a collective sense; and when using it in the most extensive signification, the adjacent isles including that of Van Diemen, must be understood to be comprehended.' [Footnote]: 'Had I permitted myself any innovation upon the original term, it would have been to convert it into Australia; as being more agreeable to the ear, and of an assimilation to the names of the other great portions of the earth.'

AUSTRALIAN FLAG Hot climate and country work have brought in a fashion among bushmen of wearing a belt or leather strap round the top of trousers instead of braces. This often causes a fold in the shirt protruding all round from under the waistcoat, which is playfully known as 'the Australian flag.'

BACK-BLOCKS (1) The far interior of Australia, and away from settled country. Land in Australia is divided on the survey maps into blocks, a word confined, in England and the United States, to town lands; (2) The parts of a station distant from the frontage.

BANKER a river full up to the top of the banks.

BARCOO ROT a disease infecting inhabitants of various parts of the interior of Australia, but chiefly bushmen. It consists of persistent ulceration of the skin, chiefly on the back of the hands, and often originating in abrasions. It is attributed to monot-
ony of diet and to the cloudless climate, with its alternations of extreme cold at night and burning heat by day. It is said to be maintained and aggravated by the irritation of small flies.

BLACK-BIRDING kidnapping natives of South Sea islands for service in Queensland plantations.

BLACK-TRACKER an aboriginal employed in tracking criminals.

BULLSWOOL colloquial name for the inner portion of the covering of the stringy bark tree. This is a dry finely fibrous substance, easily disintegrated by rubbing between the hands. It forms a valuable tinder for kindling a fire in the bush, and is largely employed for that purpose. It is not unlike the matted hair of a bull, and is reddish in colour, hence, perhaps this nickname.

BUSTER, SOUTHERLY the word is a corruption of 'burster,' that which bursts. A sudden and violent squall from the south. The name, used first in Sydney, has been adopted also in other Australian cities.

CATTLE-DUFFER a man who steals cattle (usually by altering their brands).

COCKATOO (1) Bird-name. (2) A small farmer ... The name was originally given in contempt ... but it is now used by farmers themselves. *Cocky* is a common abbreviation.

COCK-EYED BOB a local slang term in Western Australia for a thunderstorm.

CORNSTALK a young man or girl born and bred in New South Wales, especially if tall and big.

CURRENCY obsolete name for those colonially-born.

1827. P Cunningham, 'Two Years in New South Wales,' vol. ii, p. 33:
'Our colonial-born brethren are best known here by the name of Currency, in contradistinction to Sterling, or those born in the mother-country. The name was originally given by a facetious paymaster of the 73rd Regiment quartered here – the pound currency being at that time inferior to the pound sterling.'

DAMPER a large scone of flour and water baked in hot ashes; the bread of the bush, which is always unleavened.

DILLY-BAG an aboriginal word, coming from Queensland, for a bag made either of grasses or of fur twisted into a cord ... and the word is used by bushmen for a little bag for odds and ends.

DOWN a prejudice against, hostility to; a peculiarly Australian noun made out of the adverb.

1856. W. W. Dobie, 'Recollections of a Visit to Port Phillip,' p. 84:
'... the bushranger had been in search of another squatter, on whom "he said he had a down" ...'

DROVE to drive travelling cattle or sheep.

ECHIDNA a fossorial [digging or burrowing] Monotreme, in general appearance resembling a Porcupine, and often called *Spiny Ant-eater* or *Porcupine*, or *Porcupine Ant-eater*.

FLYING-FOX a gigantic Australian bat.

FREE-SELECTOR one who takes up a block of Crown land under the Land Laws and by annual payments acquires the freehold.

GIDGEE aboriginal word of New South Wales and Queensland for a species of *Acacia*.

GIN a native word for an aboriginal woman.

GULLY a narrow valley. The word is very common in Australia, and is frequently used as a placename.

GULLY-RAKER a long whip.

GUM-TREE the popular name for any tree of the various species of *Eucalyptus*.

HUMPY a native hut.

HUON-PINE a large Tasmanian evergreen tree.

IRONBARK early settlers gave this name to several large Eucalypts, from the hardness of their bark.

JACKAROO a name for a ... young man fresh from England, learning squatting.

KOALA aboriginal name for the native bear.

KOOKABURRA the aboriginal name for the bird called [by settlers] the 'Laughing Jackass'.

LARRIKIN the word has various shades of meaning between a playful youngster and a blackguardly rough.

LUBRA aboriginal name for a black woman.

MESSAGE-STICK the aboriginals sometimes carve little blocks of wood with various marks to convey messages. These are called by the whites *message-sticks*.

MOB a large number, the Australian noun of multitude, and not implying anything low or noisy.

MULGA an aboriginal word ... given to various species of *Acacia*.

NUGGETTY applied to a horse or a man. Short, thick-set and strong.

NULLA-NULLA a battle club of the aborigines in Australia.

PATRIOT humorously applied to convicts.

PLATYPUS a remarkable Monotreme, in shape like a Mole, with a bill like a Duck. Hence its other names of *Duck-bill* or *Duck-mole*.

PUSH a gang. The word is of late very common in Australia. It was once a prison term ... In Thieves' English a *push* is – (1) a crowd; (2) an association for a particular robbery. In Australia, its use ... spread until it now often means a clique, set, party, and even jocularly so far as 'the Government House Push.'

QUART-POT TEA Explained in quotation [also known as *billy tea*].

1885. H. Finch-Hatton, 'Advance Australia,' p. 111:

'"Quart-pot" tea, as tea made in the bush always called, is really the proper way to make it ... The tea is really made with boiling water, which brings out its full flavour, and it is drunk before it has time to draw too much.'

REMITTANCE-MAN one who derives the means of an inglorious and frequently dissolute existence from the periodical receipt of money sent out to him from Europe.

ROUSEABOUT a station-hand put on to any work, a Jack of all work, an 'odd job man.'

SCRUBBER a bullock that has taken to the scrub and so become wild. Also *Scrub-cattle*.

SLUSHER OR SLUSHY cook's assistant at shearing-time on a station.

SUNDOWNER a tramp who takes care to arrive at a station at sundown, so that he shall be provided with 'tucker' at the squatter's cost: one of those who goes about the country seeking work and devoutly hoping they may not find it.

TASMANIAN TIGER also called *Native Wolf*, *Marsupial Wolf*, *Zebra Wolf*, and *Hyena*; genus *Thylacinus*. It is the largest carnivorous marsupial extant, and is so much like a *wolf* in appearance that it well deserves its vernacular name of Wolf, though now-a-days it is generally called Tiger.

VERANDAH In Australia, the heat of the sun makes verandahs much commoner than in England. They are an architectural feature of all dwelling-houses in suburb or bush, and of most City shops, where they render the broad side-walks an almost continuous arcade. 'Under the Verandah' has acquired the meaning 'where city men most do congregate.'

WALLABY TRACK, ON THE Tramping the country on foot, looking for work. Often in the bush the only perceptible tracks by which the scrub can be penetrated, are the tracks worn down by the wallaby ... These tracks may lead to water or they may be aimless and rambling. Thus the man '*on the wallaby*' may be looking for food or for work, or aimlessly wandering by day and getting food and shelter as a *Sundowner* at night.

WILLY WILLY native name for a storm in the North-west of Australia.

9

THE 'BANJO' AND *THE BULLETIN*

On 31 January 1880, two journalists, John Haynes and John Feltham Archibald, started a weekly paper they called *The Bulletin*. These two were not what you might call modest men – they were not the type to look down at their shoes, and shuffle their feet, and hope shyly that you rather like their new publication. Instead, the first issue contained this bold statement:

> The aim of the proprietors is to establish a journal which cannot be beaten – excellent in the illustrations which embellish its pages and unsurpassed in the vigor, freshness and geniality of its literary contributors. To this end, the services of the best men in the realm of pen and pencil in the colony

have been secured, and, fair support conceded, *The Bulletin*
will assuredly become the best and most interesting newspaper
published in Australia.

There was more bluff and bluster than serious planning in those
words, and the publication struggled in its early days. But in
time it became all that those confident words suggested and
more. What *The Bulletin* actually became was an encourager of
Australian writing and (as such) a celebration of the Australian
language.

It encouraged its readers to become its contributors. And
as its reputation, and its circulation, spread the contributions
began to pour in – paragraphs, anecdotes and attempts at verse
– many, perhaps written with 'a thumbnail dipped in tar', just
as Clancy's shearing mate wrote to Andrew Barton Paterson,
the young solicitor.

Paterson first appeared in the pages of *The Bulletin* under
the penname of 'The Banjo' (the name of one his favourite
horses). And it was JF Archibald (editor from April 1886) who
discovered and nurtured Paterson's talent. To this day Paterson
remains Australia's bestselling poet. He is the author of both
our best-known and best-loved bush ballad ('The Man from
Snowy River') and our best-known and best-loved song ('Waltzing Matilda').

Writing about his discoverer, Paterson said of Archibald:

Cynic and pessimist as he was he never lost faith in the
ultimate success of Australians, and when in the process of time
his name is forgotten and people ask, 'Who was this Archibald
who left this bequest?' the question can be answered by saying:

'He was the first man who believed in the home-made Australian article.'

Archibald (in later years his changed his Christian names to the rather more artistic-sounding Jules François) gave Australia the Archibald art prize for portraiture and gave the city of Sydney the Archibald Fountain (in Hyde Park). But perhaps more important than either of those: in *The Bulletin* he gave the Australian language confidence and self-expression.

Archibald's first letter to a young AB Paterson captures the breadth of his vision and his tone of confidence:

> I want you to remember that Australia is a big place and
> I want you to write the stuff that will appeal not only to
> Sydney people, but that will be of interest to the pearler up at
> Thursday Island and the farmer down in Victoria. On all public
> questions the press are apt to sing in chorus. If you go to a
> concert you may hear a man sing in discord which is put there
> by the composer, and that discord catches the ear over the
> voices of the chorus. Well, don't be afraid to sing the discord.
> Even if you are wrong, you will have drawn attention to what
> you want to say.

The Bulletin really flowered in the 1890s, a time when the business heart of Australia was in Melbourne ('Marvellous Melbourne', grown by a real estate boom, driven by gold) and all the colonies were drawing together to become a nation.

This is Paterson's description of his first visit to the *Bulletin* offices and his first meeting with Archibald:

Off I went and climbed a grimy flight of stairs at 24 Pitt Street, until I stood before a door marked, 'Mr Archibald, editor'. On the door was pinned a spirited drawing of a gentleman lying quite loose on the string with a dagger through him, and on the drawing was written: 'Archie, this is what will happen to you if you don't use my drawing about the policeman.' It cheered me up a lot. Evidently this was a free-and-easy place.

The drawing on the door is a reminder that *The Bulletin* was also, for many years, home to Australia's best cartoonists and black-and-white artists.

But it was the language that mattered. It was nicknamed 'the bushman's bible' because it was avidly read around campfires, in settlers' huts and in shearing sheds during smoko. And many of those who read also contributed.

In her 1979 history of *The Bulletin* Patricia Rolfe writes:

> After 1886 a regular notice was published, calling for contributions – original humorous or political matter, unpublished anecdotes, humorous poems, serious poems, and short Australian stories. Length was stipulated, eight to 50 lines preferred for poems: up to 3,000 words for stories, but half that length was preferred. Another stock notice ran: Every man can write at least one book; every man with brains has at least one good story to tell; every man with or without brains, moves in a different circle and knows things unknown to any other man ... mail your work to *The Bulletin*, which pays for accepted matter.
>
> Archibald's constant stricture was, Boil it down. 'Don't write a column on any subject if a half-column will do,' the paper would advise. 'Don't write half a column where a mere paragraph is enough.'

And the paragraphs came flooding in – up to a thousand contributions a week. Only a handful, of course, ended up in print, but those few were important because they spoke with a genuine Australian accent: they employed the rich and colourful dialect that the Australian language had become.

On 28 February 1885, Banjo Paterson made his first appearance in the pages of *The Bulletin* with a short poem. On 22 December 1888, Henry Lawson's first story, 'His Father's Mate', was published. In the same issue Paterson's first true bush ballad appeared: 'Old Pardon, the Son of Reprieve' (the first of many ballads he would write about horses and horsemen). And all the time the modest paragraphs, yarns and bits of verse by 'bush scribblers' kept appearing.

Decades later in *The Australian Language* (1966), Sidney J Baker could write:

> The simple facts are that the material on bush lore, slang and idiom, collected by thousands of writers in *The Bulletin* pages is absolutely irreplaceable ... Of course, the quality of it varied. A good deal of *The Bulletin* material looks as though it had been carved out of the Australian environment with a bush-hook and not a pen, but good or bad the great bulk of it provides a magnificent glimpse of the Australia so few Australians appreciate. What in a few issues of the journal might appear trivial and unessential nonsense falls into its place over the period of half a century like a minute part of an immense jigsaw puzzle.

(Just what Sid Baker made of that puzzle we'll see in chapter 14.)

Along with Banjo Paterson and Henry Lawson (and those rough bush scribblers described by Baker) many other writers, using the Australian dialect with power and imagination, appeared in the pages of *The Bulletin*: Joseph Furphy, Barcroft Boake, 'Breaker' Morant, Barbara Baynton, Louis Becke, Christopher Brennan, Victor Daley, CJ Dennis, Miles Franklin, Mary Gilmore, Will Ogilvie, WT Goodge, John O'Brien, Kenneth Slessor and Thomas E Spencer, to name a randomly selected few among many.

The Scottish poet Robbie Burns (1759–96) was much admired for his dialect verse (*Poems Chiefly in the Scottish Dialect* was published in 1786) and Archibald seemed intent on developing verse (and prose) written in the Australian dialect. The point of this for our story is that Aussie English was now showing its vigour, its colour and its inventive turn of phrase in print – and ordinary Australian readers were loving it. It quickly became clear that they were very keen about a popular literature that spoke the same language they did.

How much they loved it we can see by focusing on just one of those *Bulletin* writers – AB 'Banjo' Paterson, the most famous of them all.

Andrew Barton Paterson was born at Narrambla, near Orange (New South Wales) on 17 February 1864. He was named Andrew after his father, and to avoid confusion was always known in the family by his middle name – usually as 'Barty'. His father had a station called Buckinbar at Obley, near Yeoval in the Western District of New South Wales. It was poor land held on lease from the Crown at a few pence an acre.

Barty's mother Rose (née Barton) was sent to Narrambla (owned by Rose's aunt and uncle) for the birth of her son because it was nearer to Orange (on the Orange–Ophir road, about two and a half miles north-east of the town) and hence closer to suitable medical help should the birth prove difficult. Barty was the first child born to Andrew and Rose, and when the family was complete he had five younger sisters and one brother: Florence, Jessie, Edith, Grace, Gwen and Hamilton.

In 1870, when Barty was six, the family moved from Buckinbar to a station called Illalong in the Yass district, on the main route between Sydney and Melbourne (Barty grew up familiar with the sight of horsemen, bullock teams and Cobb & Co coaches on the dirt track that was the 'main road'). The gold diggings at Lambing Flat (now Young) were only a day's ride away, and the gold escort came past twice a week with an armed trooper riding in front, and another on the box with the coachman.

His family was cultivated and well read, and Barty was well taught in the home when he was young. Once he was able to catch a horse in the home paddock he was sent each day (riding bareback) to the little bush school at Binalong (a 'two-pub town' famous for the fact that the bushranger John Gilbert was buried in the police paddock).

Paterson went to school with the young descendants of John Dunn – another bushranger, made famous by the folk song 'Dunn, Gilbert and Ben Hall'. (Many years later, when he was a grandfather, Paterson wrote about his memories of growing up in the bush in the delightful book *Illalong Children*.)

In 1874, when he was ten, young Barty was sent to further his education at Sydney Grammar School. He lived with his grandmother Emily Barton in her house at Gladesville (the house, called Rockend, is still standing), and went to school each day by ferry (travelling with his Uncle Frank, a well-known Sydney solicitor). Grandma Emily was a cultured woman who moved in literary and musical circles, and she entertained Barty with gripping (and sometimes grim) stories about her early life as the young wife of a pioneer squatter.

He made friends at school, did well in his studies, and excelled at sports, but he spent all his holidays at Illalong (which he continued to do for as long as his family lived there). He spent these holidays working with the stockmen on the station (which no longer belonged to his father – he was employed as manager when he had to sell Illalong to pay his debts). During these working holidays Paterson developed even further his already considerable skills as a horseman and listened to old bush songs and old bush yarns.

In 1880 Barty matriculated from Sydney Grammar School and became an articled clerk at a firm of Sydney solicitors – doing their clerical work by day, and studying law by night. Later he became managing clerk to a law firm that handled the business of several banks (and saw, in the process, what the banks could do to small property holders).

He was only twenty-one when (in 1885) his first verses were published in *The Bulletin*. In the following year he was admitted to the Roll of Solicitors, and began to practise as a lawyer (from 28 August 1886). But he never enjoyed the law as a profession, longed to be a writer, and escaped from the dusty law office as soon as it was possible to do so.

At the end of 1888 the now 24-year-old Paterson saw his first significant bush ballad, 'Old Pardon, the Son of Reprieve', appear in *The Bulletin*. Earlier in that same year he met Henry Lawson, and later did some law work for him (representing him in publishing contracts). They were friendly, but never close friends (Paterson being quiet and reserved and unlike the heavy-drinking Lawson in character). Contrary to popular misconception, however, Paterson and Lawson were never antagonistic. (Their famous 'battle in verse' in the pages of *The Bulletin* was something the two of them cooked up to help them make more sales!)

In 1889 Paterson published his legendary bush ballad, 'Clancy of the Overflow', in *The Bulletin*. A year later, now aged 26, he published the greatest of his bush ballads, 'The Man from Snowy River', in *The Bulletin* – not based, he explained, on any one individual, but on the mountain riders he had met as a young man. 'It was written,' he later wrote, 'to describe the cleaning up of the wild horses in my own district … I had to create a character, to imagine a man who would ride better than anybody else, and where else would he come from except from the Snowy?'

In January 1895 (about to turn 31) Paterson went to visit Sarah Riley (his fiancée at the time) at Winton in Queensland. The pair travelled out to Dagworth Station where they met the manager Bob Macpherson and his sister Christina. It was Bob Macpherson who introduced Paterson to the Queensland expression *waltzing matilda* ('carrying a swag'), and rode with him to Combo waterhole where they found the remains of a sheep that had been killed (and partly cooked and eaten) by a passing swaggie. Bob also told Barty about the shearers' strike of the previous year which had ended with one the shearers (one of the strike leaders) committing suicide.

Back at the Dagworth homestead Christina Macpherson played on her autoharp (an instrument a bit like a zither) a tune called 'Craigielee' (which she had heard played by a brass band at the Warrnambool races, Victoria, the previous year). Paterson wrote words to go with this tune, incorporating all those elements: Combo waterhole, the swaggie, the sheep, the suicide, and *waltzing matilda*. Thus was written his most famous bush ballad (and Australia's best-loved song).

In October 1895 Angus & Robertson published *The Man from Snowy River and Other Verses* with an introduction by Rolf Boldrewood. The book was an immediate bestseller (and has a remained a bestseller ever since). The first print run sold out in a month. The book has by now sold (it is estimated) in excess of 200 000 copies.

In later years 'The Man from Snowy River' became the inspiration for two movies, a television series and an arena spectacular. And the bush ballads of Banjo Paterson continue to appear, year after year, in new editions – often illustrated to capture the imagination of younger readers.

The point of all this for our story is what it demonstrates about the confidence Australians had in their own language – their own distinctive dialect – even before the colonies had come together to form a nation. Of course there had been an Australian literature, and published use of Aussie English, before *The Bulletin*, but the determination of JF Archibald to encourage something distinctively Australian in language and tone, and the weekly nature of its publication, made *The Bulletin* an important watershed in the celebration of the Australian language in print.

Aussie English was now proving itself (in print) to be an expressive, brash language, full of clever new coinages, making creative new uses of old words and generating a popular literature.

Furthermore, the new coinages constantly springing up in the Australian dialect were no longer coming only from the bush: the streets of Australian cities were now breeding grounds for new words and phrases – especially the crowded back streets where the working classes lived. It's their words and phrases we meet next.

WORD LIST

For those who want to know more about *The Bulletin* and its colourful history, the story can be found in *The Journalistic Javelin* by Patricia Rolfe. And there are three standard biographies of Banjo Paterson: *The Banjo of the Bush* by Clement Semmler, *Poet by Accident* by Colin Roderick and *Banjo* by Paul Terry.

Below are some words found in *The Collected Verse of A. B. Paterson*, which brought together his three bestselling volumes: *The Man from Snowy River*, *Rio Grande* and *Saltbush Bill J. P.*

From Aussie words and placenames such as those listed below, Paterson was able to weave strong, rhythmic verse that told gripping tales that could move tough bush workers to laughter or tears.

CASTLEREAGH RIVER (NEW SOUTH WALES) named by GW Evans during Oxley's expedition of 1818 in honour of Lord Castlereagh, British Secretary of State for the Colonies: 'It is the land of lots o' time along the Castlereagh' ('The Travelling Post Office').

COME-BY-CHANCE this placename was given by George and William Colles in 1862 when they found (to their surprise)

that they were able to purchase a sheep station in this district
(some 57 kilometres south-east of Walgett); the name so
delighted Paterson when he came across it that it inspired its
own bush ballad: 'But my languid mood forsook me, when I
found a name that took me; / Quite by chance I came across
it – 'Come-by-Chance' was what I read ...'.

COOPER CREEK flowing from the Gulf Country of
Queensland into South Australia, this watercourse was named
by explorer Charles Sturt in 1845 in honour of Sir Charles
Cooper, the first South Australian Chief Justice. Paterson
calls it just 'the Cooper' and he pictures Clancy 'Gone
a-droving "down the Cooper" where the Western drovers go'.

CRACK 'all the cracks had gathered to the fray' (in 'The Man
from Snowy River') – a crack being someone who was a very
good at something; the *Australian National Dictionary* says this is
probably a specialised use of an English dialect word (originally it
seems to have meant boasting, then that which is boasted about,
and then the one who has something worth boasting about).

DROVE The *Australian National Dictionary* says 'not
exclusively Australian, but of local significance' – much used
by Paterson; for instance 'In the Droving Days', a ballad
about an old horse bought at auction: 'For though he scarcely
a trot can raise / He can take me back to the droving days'.

GEEBUNG a wild fruit tree or shrub of the genus *Persoonia*;
Paterson gave this name to a fictional outback town he
invented for one of his best-known comic bush ballads: 'It was
somewhere up the country, in a land of rock and scrub / That
they formed an institution called the Geebung Polo Club'.

IRONBARK Paterson took the name of this type of eucalypt and used it as the name of a fictional outback town in 'The Man from Ironbark'.

KURRAJONG a tree, *Brachychiton populneus*, widespread in eastern Australia where it was valued as fodder; from the Dharuk word *garajung* 'fishing line' (it was applied to the tree from whose bark fishing lines were generally made): 'Where mountain ash and kurrajong grew wide' ('The Man from Snowy River').

MATE Australian English made special use of this word from British English to mean friend, partner, comrade, chum, fellow-worker – with the implication of a level of loyalty and reliability. The notion of 'mateship' is especially associated with another *Bulletin* writer, Henry Lawson, but there are references in Paterson as well: the note that is quoted *verbatim* in 'Clancy of the Overflow' was written by 'his shearing mate'.

MIMOSA a tangled, spiny shrub or small tree, *Acacia farnesiana*; in 'The Man from Snowy River' they found the wild bush horses 'by the big mimosa clump'.

MOUNTAIN ASH a type of eucalypt: 'Where mountain ash and kurrajong grew wide' (in 'The Man from Snowy River').

NARROMINE a New South Wales placename taken from the Aboriginal word *gnarrowmine*, meaning 'place of honey': 'The stranger came from Narromine and made his little joke; / 'They say we folks in Narromine are narrow-minded folks ...' ('City of Dreadful Thirst').

NEVER-NEVER the far interior of Australia; the remote outback; sometimes shortened to just 'the Never', as in 'They bred him out back on the "Never"' ('Old Pardon, the Son of Reprieve').

OVERFLOW, THE the name of a fictional outback sheep and cattle station; in full Overflow Station; a name along the same lines as Illalong Station, Buckinbar Station, Narrambla Station, Dagworth Station, and other sheep and cattle stations (perhaps Paterson pictured it as a Darling River station, dependent on the annual flooding of that river for its pastures).

OVERLAND to take stock across the country; celebrated in the folk-song 'The Overlanders' (included by Paterson in his anthology *Old Bush Songs*) and occurring often in the ballads – for instance in the name of the character 'Saltbush Bill, the king of the overland'.

POUND the 'colt from old Regret' (in 'The Man from Snowy River') was 'worth a thousand pound' – it was a commonplace of conversational Aussie English when the pound was a unit of currency to always use the singular no matter how many pounds were being spoken about, as in 'it's worth five pound' (or, in the case of the horse, a thousand pound).

SALTBUSH the wild alkaline herb or shrub, growing on the interior plains of Australia, on which horses and sheep feed; the term occurs often in Paterson's verse – for example in the name of the character 'Saltbush Bill, the king of the overland'.

SHEARING clipping the fleece from a sheep; not exclusively an Australian word, but with a special resonance here, as in 'He was shearing when I knew him, so I sent the letter to him ...' ('Clancy of the Overflow').

STRINGYBARK any of a group of species of the genus *Eucalyptus* with a characteristic tough fibrous bark: 'Through the stringybarks and saplings, on the rough and broken ground ...' ('The Man from Snowy River').

WALTZING MATILDA How did carrying a swag come be *a-waltzing matilda*? Quite possibly from the German community in South Australia. *Matilda* was a common German word for girlfriend – just the like the Irish *sheila*. And if your girlfriend/fiancée/wife wasn't around you turned to your blanket or bed-roll for warmth and comfort. *Waltz* is also German – originally with the meaning of going round and round in a dance, but then it was applied to any other aimless or circular travels. But it was in Australia that these two words were put together– quite possibly in the melting pot of the goldfields.

10

LARRIKIN LINGO

Our dialect by this time was robust and dynamic with a hearty laugh – as subtle as a troop of cavalry galloping over a tin bridge. It was time for this language to have its own name. And for that it needed a nation to belong to.

The nation of Australia was born on 1 January 1901. There had been murmurings about the possibility of forming a federation of the colonies since quite early in the nineteenth century, but there was little popular or political support until the 1880s when a passion for nationhood began to bloom. A Federal Council of Australasia was formed – a kind of talk-fest to discuss the possibilities and work out what should be in a constitution.

However, the richest and most heavily populated colony, New South Wales, held back – fearing a loss of power from sharing with the other colonies, and fearing rivalry from gold-rich, booming Victoria. It was the Premier of New South Wales, Sir Henry Parkes, who turned this attitude around (and by doing so earned the title of 'the Father of Federation').

A series of constitutional conventions was held (beginning in 1891) that eventually produced a draft constitution. In 1898 referendums were held in New South Wales, Victoria, South Australia and Tasmania, recording a 'Yes' majority in each colony, but in New South Wales the 'Yes' majority was not big enough to carry the referendum. There were further referendums in 1899. This time Queensland was included, and the vote was finally carried in New South Wales.

In 1900 the British Parliament passed the *Commonwealth of Australia Constitution Act* (and Western Australia held its own referendum and voted to join with the other colonies). The result was the celebration of the birth of the new nation on 1 January 1901 – with the first Federal Parliament being opened by the Duke of York, in Melbourne, on 9 May that year.

So it came about that the Australian language now had a nation to speak for. And in that new nation the cities were booming and Aussie English was taking off in new directions. What was needed was a writer with an ear to pick up these developments, and record and celebrate them. The writer who answered that call was CJ Dennis.

Clarence James Dennis was born in 1876 in Auburn, South Australia. As a boy he was known as Clarrie, but he seems to have disliked both his given names and as an adult was addressed either by his initials or by the nickname 'Den'. His father was a publican, running pubs first in Auburn and then in nearby Laura. Den's mother died in 1890 when he was fourteen and for the next few years he was raised by four of his aunts (his mother's sisters). Den came from an Irish Catholic family, and for a while attended a Christian Brothers college in Adelaide.

On leaving school he worked briefly as a solicitor's clerk, and then became a journalist – joining the staff of the Adelaide paper *The Critic* (described by his biographer as a 'sedate little social weekly'). He seems to have left after a year or so, working briefly for his father as a bartender, and then going on the road, doing odd jobs here and there. But in the year that the new nation of Australia was born he was back in Adelaide and back on the staff of *The Critic*.

Den and several other young staff members of *The Critic* left that publication to start their own weekly satirical journal, which they called *The Gadfly*. The venture was not a success and Den drifted off to Melbourne looking for work as a freelance journalist. Down on his luck, he moved out to Toolangi – an isolated timber settlement near Healesville, north-east of Melbourne. He kept writing, as 'occupational therapy' to stop himself becoming depressed. The result was his first collection of verse: *Backblock Ballads and Other Verse*, published by Coles Book Arcade of Melbourne in 1913.

The book was not a notable success, but it contained four verse stories about a character Den called 'the Sentimental Bloke'. Den could see their potential, and wrote more ballads about the same character, which he sold to *The Bulletin*. When he had fourteen ballads about 'the Bloke' and the love of his life (Doreen) he offered them to Angus & Robertson. The resulting book was published in 1915 as *The Songs of a*

Sentimental Bloke with illustrations by *Bulletin* cartoonist Hal Gye. This turned out to be an overwhelming success, selling some 50 000 copies in the first few years.

What is distinctive about *The Sentimental Bloke* is the language. Den wrote about his memorable characters using the form of Aussie English spoken in the backstreets of inner Melbourne. This, for example, is how the Bloke describes his meeting with Doreen:

> 'Er name's Doreen ... Well, spare me bloomin' days!
> You could er knocked me down wiv 'arf a brick!
> Yes, me, that kids meself I know their ways,
> An' 'as a name for smoogin' in our click!
> I just lines up an' tips the saucy wink.
> But strike! The way she piled on dawg! Yer'd think
> A bloke was givin' back-chat to the Queen ...
> 'Er name's Doreen.

> I seen 'er in the market first uv all,
> Inspectin' brums at Steeny Isaac's stall.
> I backs me barrer in – the same ole way –
> An' sez, 'Wot O! It's been a bonzer day.
> 'Ow is it fer a walk?'... Oh, 'oly wars!
> The sorter look she gimme! Jest becors
> I tried to chat 'er, like you'd make a start
> Wiv any tart.

Despite this inauspicious beginning the romance blossoms and the Bloke (his name is Bill, although he's also known as 'the Kid') sees off a rival ('the stror 'at coot') and wins Doreen's hand in marriage. The book ends with the birth of their first child and the little family settled on a market garden just outside Melbourne. The characters are engaging and the stories are well told – but it's the language that's striking: so striking, in fact, as to require a glossary at the back of the book.

Den followed up *The Songs of a Sentimental Bloke* with more books of verse in the same vernacular: *The Moods of Ginger Mick* (in which Bill's mate Ginger Mick joins the army to fight in the 'big stoush' and dies at Gallipoli) and two books which developed minor characters from the earlier stories, *Rose of Spadgers* and *Digger Smith*.

Any dialect which is sufficiently lively, colourful and vigorous is bound to generate its own dialect literature. And the dialect verse of CJ Dennis is another example of Aussie English doing exactly that.

Australian Prime Minister Joe Lyons described Dennis as 'the Robert Burns of Australia' – comparing him to the great Scottish dialect poet. The form of Aussie English Dennis employed came from an inner-city group known as 'larrikins'. So, in looking at their language a good place to start might be with that word.

Here's what EE Morris had to say about *larrikin* in his *Dictionary of Austral English:*

> **larrikin,** *n.* The word has various shades of meaning between
> a playful youngster and a blackguardly rough. Little street boys
> are often in a kindly way called little *larrikins* ... Archibald
> Forbes described the larrikin as 'a cross between the Street
> Arab and the Hoodlum, with a dash of the Rough thrown in to
> improve the mixture.'...

There are three views as to the origin of the word, viz. –

(1) That it is a phonetic spelling of the broad Irish pronunciation, with a trilled *r* of the word *larking*. The story goes that a certain Sergeant Dalton, about the year 1869, charged a youthful prisoner at the Melbourne Police Court with being *'a-larrakin'* about in the streets.' The Police Magistrate, Mr. Sturt, did not quite catch the word – 'A what, Sergeant?' – 'A larrikin', your Worchup.' The police court reporter used the word the next day in the paper, and it stuck …

This story is believed by 99 persons out of 100; unfortunately it lacks confirmation; for the record of the incident cannot be discovered, after long search in files by many people. Mr. Skeat's warning must be remembered – 'As a rule, derivations which require a story to be told turn out to be false.'

(2) That the word is thieves' English, promoted like *swag*, *plant*, *lift* etc., into ordinary Australian English. Warders testify that for a number of years before the word appeared in print, it was used among criminals in jail as two separate words, viz. – *leary* ('cute, fly, knowing), and *kinchen* (youngster), – *'leary kinchen,'* – shortened commonly into *'leary kin'* and *'leary kid'*. Australian warders and constables are Irish, almost to a man. Their pronunciation of *'leary kin'* would be very nearly *'lairy kin'* which becomes the single word *larrikin* … It is possible that Sergeant Dalton used this expression and was misunderstood by the reporter.

(3) The word has been derived from the French *larron* (a thief), which is from the Latin *latronem* (a robber). This became in English *larry*, to which the English diminutive, *kin*, was added; although this etymology is always derided in Melbourne.

All of which is very inventive. Unfortunately Morris omits the simplest (but most likely) explanation, namely, that *larrikin* is another of those English dialect words adopted in Australia (which then survived here after the original died out in the British Isles). The source seems to be a Warwickshire and Worcestershire word meaning 'a mischievous youth'.

Much of the language used by larrikins was ordinary Aussie English (especially the slang terms common at the time). But some of it was distinctive. So how did CJ Dennis learn this distinctive larrikin lingo? Here's the answer given by his biographer Alec Chisholm:

> The explanation seems to be, in part at any rate, that Dennis had an unusually alert ear and eye for picturesque words and phrases, and was a keen, if casual, snapper-up of unconsidered trifles of the kind. As early as August of 1913 (two years before *The Sentimental Bloke* was published) he revealed in a letter … that he had long been collecting words for a Dictionary of Slang which he meditated producing, and had then assembled about seven hundred words. But by that time, he said, he had 'gone rather cold' on the project, for the collecting of the material was 'slogging sort of work'.

There is also some evidence that Dennis drew on some of the larrikin lingo recorded by Louis Stone in his novel *Jonah* (set in the inner suburbs of Sydney) published in 1911. Chisholm points out that both writers refer to larrikins as 'blokes' and 'cobbers' who 'poke borak' and 'chiack' and 'chuck off'; who wear dashing 'clobber'; who get into trouble with 'Johns' and other 'cows'; and who exclaim at intervals 'ribuck,' 'fair dinkum', 'blimey', 'strewth' and 'my oath'.

To see such language in action, here's how 'the Bloke' reacts when his dreaded rival 'the stror 'at coot' comes on the scene, seeking to steal Doreen's affections:

> Ar, wimmin! Wot a blinded fool I've been!
> I arsts meself, wot else could I ixpeck?
> I done me block complete on this Doreen,
> An' now me 'eart is broke, me life's a wreck!
> The dreams I dreamed, the dilly thorts I thunk
> Is up the pole, an' joy 'as done a bunk.
>   ...
>
> I took a derry on this stror 'at coot
> First time I seen 'im dodgin' round Doreen.
> 'Im, wiv 'is giddy tie an' Yankee soot,
> Ferever yappin' like a tork-machine
> About 'The Hoffis' where 'e 'ad a grip ...
> The way 'e smiled at 'er give me the pip!
>   ...

Me jealous? Jealous of that cross-eyed cow?
I set 'im cos I couldn't sight 'is face.
'Is yappin'; fair got on me nerves, some'ow.
I couldn't stand 'im 'angin' round 'er place.
A coot like that! ... But it don't matter much,
She's welkim to 'im if she fancies such.

The Sentimental Bloke has twice been turned into a movie: as a classic Australian silent film by Raymond Longford in 1919, and then as a sound movie in 1932. And it's twice become a stage show, first as a musical, then as part of a one-man show performed by John Derum, telling the story of Den's life and work: *More Than a Sentimental Bloke*.

And there's one other verse by CJ Dennis that deserves a mention in the story of Aussie English. 'The Australaise' was originally submitted as a joking entry in a national song competition conducted by *The Bulletin* in 1908. Dennis then included it in his 1913 collection *Backblock Ballads and Other Verse*. And then during the First World War, in 1915, it was reprinted as a leaflet for Australian soldiers.

'The Australaise' has two distinctive features. The first is that it can be sung to the tune of 'Onward Christian Soldiers' and the second is that it's full of blanks. The assumption made by the reader is that these blanks will be filled by 'the great Australian adjective' (bloody) but Dennis stresses that there are other options. The leaflet version carries the following note: 'Where a dash replaces a missing word, the adjective "blessed" may be interpolated. In cases demanding greater emphasis, the use of the word "blooming" is permissible. However, any other word may be used that suggests itself as suitable.'

Here are the first verse and chorus of 'The Australaise':

Fellers of Australier,
Blokes an' coves an' coots,
Shift yer – – – carcases,
Move yer – – – boots.
Gird yer – – – loins up,
Get yer – – – gun,
Set the – – – enermy
An' watch the blighters run.

Chorus
Get a – – – move on,
Have some – – – sense.
Learn the – – – art of
Self de- – – – -fence.

And that last line shows what Aussie English can do to an adjective. In fact, in chapter 15 we'll look at John O'Grady's suggestion that 'the great Australian adjective' should be regarded as 'the integrated adjective'.

But before we do, it's time for Aussie English to pull on a uniform and march off to war.

WORD LIST

There are two books that will tell you more about CJ Dennis: *The Making of a Sentimental Bloke* by Alec H Chisholm (1946) and *More than a Sentimental Bloke* by John Derum (1990) – an expanded version of the script of his one-man stage show.

At the back of *The Songs of a Sentimental Bloke* is a glossary, perhaps preserving some of Dennis's planned Dictionary of Slang. Below is a selection from that glossary (the definitions are in Den's own words).

ALLEY, TO TOSS IN THE to give up the ghost.

AR an exclamation expressing joy, sorrow, surprise, etc., according to the manner of utterance.

'ARD CASE (HARD CASE) a shrewd or humorous person.

BACK AND FILL to vacillate; to shuffle.

BEANS coins; money.

BELLERS (BELLOWS) the lungs.

BOKAYS compliments, flattery.

BOKO the nose.

BRISKET the chest.

BRUMS tawdry finery (from Brummagem – Birmingham).

CAT, TO WHIP THE to cry over spilt milk; i.e. to whip the cat that has spilt the milk.

CHEQUE, TO PASS IN ONE'S to depart this life.

CHEW, TO CHEW IT OVER; TO CHEW THE RAG to sulk; to nurse a grievance.

CLICK a clique; a 'push' (see *push* below).

CLINER young unmarried female.

COW a thoroughly unworthy, not to say despicable, person, place, thing or circumstance; *a fair cow*, an utterly obnoxious and otherwise unexpressible person, place, thing or circumstance.

CRACK HARDY to suppress emotion; to endure patiently; to keep a secret.

CROOL (CRUEL) THE PITCH to frustrate; to interfere with one's schemes or welfare.

CRUST sustenance; a livelihood.

DAWG (DOG) a contemptible person; ostentation; *to put on dog* to behave in an arrogant manner

DERRY an aversion; a feud; a dislike.

DICKIN a term signifying disgust or disbelief.

DILLY foolish; half-witted.

FINGER an eccentric or amusing person.

FLASH ostentatious; showy but counterfeit.

FLUFF, A BIT OF a young female person.

FOOT (ME FOOT) a term expressing ridicule.

GAME occupation; scheme; design.

GIZZARD the heart.

GLARSSY [SIC] the glassy eye; a glance of cold disdain; *the glassey alley* The favourite; the most admired.

GONE (FAIR GONE) overcome, as with emotion.

GRAFT work.

GRIFFIN, THE STRAIGHT the truth; secret information.

HIT THINGS UP to behave strenuously; riotously.

IMSHEE begone; retreat; to take yourself off.

JIFF a very brief period.

JOES melancholy thoughts.

JOHN a policeman.

KEEPS, FOR for ever; permanently.

KID STAKES pretence.

KIPSIE a house; the home.

LEERY vulgar; low.

LID the hat; *to dip the lid* to raise the hat.

LURK a plan of action; a regular occupation.

MAFEESH finish; I am finished.

MAG to scold or talk noisily.

MOOCH to saunter about aimlessly.

MULLOCK, TO POKE to deride; to tease.

NICK physical condition; *in good nick* in good health.

ODDS, ABOVE THE beyond the average; outside the pale.

ORFIS (OFFICE) a warning; a word of advice; a hint.

PACK, TO SEND TO THE to relegate to obscurity.

PILOT COVE a clergyman.

PLUG ALONG, TO to proceed doggedly.

POLE, UP THE distraught through anger, fear, etc; also, disappeared, vanished.

PUSH a company of rowdy fellows.

RAIN, TO KEEP OUT OF THE to avoid danger; to act with caution.

SCHOOL a club; a clique of gamblers, or others.

SIGHT to tolerate; to permit; also, to see; observe.

SLATS the ribs.

SOOL to attack; to urge on.

SPARE ME DAYS a pious ejaculation.

SQUARE AN' ALL of a truth; verily.

STOUSH to punch with the fists; violence.

SWANK affectation; ostentation.

TART a young woman (contraction of *sweetheart*).

TOGS clothes.

TOUGH LUCK misfortune.

UMPTY indefinite numeral.

WASTER a reprobate; an utterly useless and unworthy person.

WATERWORKS, TO TURN ON THE to shed tears.

11

DIGGER
DIALECTS

Aussie English was about to be told to pull itself together and show what it could really do. War will do that to a language.

On 18 June 1914, Archduke Ferdinand of Austria was assassinated in Sarajevo (then the capital of the Austro-Hungarian Empire's province of Bosnia). The assassin had ties to a terrorist organisation in Serbia, Austria-Hungary believed Serbia was behind the assassination, and therefore declared war on Serbia.

This action sparked the outbreak of the First World War (also known as the Great War and World War I). When fighting began France, Great Britain and Russia (known as the Allies) backed Serbia. They were opposed by the Central Powers: Austria-Hungary and Germany.

It was Germany that won the early victories in Europe. France and Britain halted the German advance on the Western Front on 14 September 1914, and for the next three and a half years the conflict bogged down in trenches that stretched across Belgium and north-eastern France.

In November 1914 Turkey entered the war (on the side of the Central Powers) when Turkish ships bombarded Russian ports on the Black Sea. From here fighting spread throughout the territories of the Ottoman Empire – the Arabian Peninsula, Palestine and Syria.

In August 1914 the Prime Minister of Australia, Joseph Cook, had accepted Britain's declaration of war as binding on Australia. He was in the midst of an election campaign at the time, but immediately offered to provide an expeditionary force of 20 000 Australian soldiers as well at putting the Australian navy under the command of the British Admiralty.

The election was won by his opponent, Labor leader Andrew Fisher, who endorsed these commitments and pledged Australian support 'to the last man and the last shilling'. The Inspector-General of the Australian Army, Brigadier-General WT Bridges, raised an all-volunteer force called the Australian Imperial Force (commonly known as the AIF).

And that was the sequence of events that led Aussie English to march off to war in the khaki uniforms of the 1st AIF.

Australia's first task, in combination with a New Zealand force, was to capture the German colonies in the South Pacific: German New Guinea, the Carolines, Nauru and Samoa, accomplished during September 1914.

Then in November 1914 an expeditionary force left Australia consisting of the 1st Division of the AIF, three Light Horse brigades, an engineers' unit and a field ambulance unit. They were joined overseas by men of the 1st New Zealand Expeditionary Force.

On 25 April 1915 the men of the combined Australian and New Zealand Army Corps (now known by its initials as ANZAC) took part in an attack on the Gallipoli peninsula in Turkey. The aim of the campaign was to allow Allied naval forces to sail through the Dardanelles and launch an attack on the Turkish capital Constantinople (now Istanbul).

The ANZAC troops landed at Anzac Cove, dug into the beaches, and fought a valiant campaign against Turkish troops who had the advantage of being above them on the cliff tops. Turkish resistance was fierce and fighting reached a stalemate. After eight costly months, the Allied forces (by then including troops from several other Commonwealth nations) were withdrawn. Australian casualties at Gallipoli were 8587 killed and 19 367 wounded.

Back home the gallantry of the Gallipoli disaster inspired the Coo-ee Marches. These began with thirty-five men who set out on a recruitment drive from Gilgandra, in New South Wales, to help in the Great War effort, calling out 'Coo-ee' to encourage men along the way to come and enlist with them. On 12 December the Coo-ee March reached Sydney with 277 men, the first of many Coo-ee recruiting marches.

And all the time Aussie English was growing and changing. Exactly why wartime produces such rapid change in language is not certain, but it has something to do with so many people being thrust together, from different walks of life, dealing with unusual circumstances. In those conditions new words and phrases are coined rapidly, some of which become permanent parts of the language after the conflict ends.

Which brings us to the story of Walter Hubert Dowling (1893–1965). He was born at Portland, Victoria, and was studying law at Queen's College, at the University of Melbourne, when war broke out. He enlisted on 30 September 1915, and served in the 57th Battalion of the AIF, spending time in Egypt before seeing active service in France. By the end of the war he was a sergeant, and had been award the Military Medal for bravery.

Dowling returned to Australia on 25 February 1919, and resumed his law studies. He graduated in 1920 and practised as a solicitor in Melbourne for most of the remainder of his life.

In 1919, while still an undergraduate, he published a book called *Digger Dialects* – a dictionary of almost 900 words and phrases used by Australians in the First World War. In his introduction he wrote: 'Australian slang is not a new thing; but in those iron years it was modified beyond recognition by the assimilation of foreign words and the formulae of novel or exotic ideas. This process of enrichment is common to every living language in all the ages.'

Digger Dialects was re-published in 1990 with additional explanatory notes by two of Australia's leading lexicographers, JM Arthur and WS Ramson. (Bill Ramson was the editor of the monumental *Australian National Dictionary* that appeared in the bicentenary year of 1988.) In their introduction to this second edition the editors say: 'Dowling was an extraordinarily acute observer of language in action – which argues a cultivated knowledge of his own and other languages … and a ready response to subtlety of nuance or other novelty.'

And by drawing on Dowling's book we can get a clear picture of what the First World War did to Aussie English.

We begin with the most significant word to emerge from the Great War: *Anzac*. As already noted, this began life as an acronym from the initial letters of the Australian and New Zealand Army Corps, and appears to have come into being (or, at least, to have been widely circulated) as the telegraphic code name for the Corps. The earliest citation is from 1915. In the first volume of CEW Bean's *Official History of Australia in the War of 1914–18* the following story appears. The setting is the Australian Army headquarters in Egypt:

> The ground-floor corridor outside the clerk's room became bordered with cases containing stationery addressed in large black stencilled letters to the 'A. and N. Z. Army Corps' ... When Wagstaff mentioned the need of a code word, one of the clerks suggested: 'How about ANZAC?' Major Wagstaff proposed the word to the general who approved of it, and 'Anzac' thereupon became the code name of the Australian and New Zealand Army Corps ... The word had already been used among the clerks. Possibly the first occasion was when Sgt. G. C. Little asked Sgt. H. V. Millington to 'throw him the ANZAC stamp'.

That, it appears, is the story of the birth of the word, recorded with Charlie Bean's typical thoroughness and precision.

But did you realise that the word *Anzac* is now copyright? So deeply has this word entered into the consciousness of our nation that there are laws, passed in 1920, to control and protect its use. The Minister for Veterans' Affairs administers the protection of the word, and the ministerial approval is needed for its use in connection with any 'trade, business, calling or profession, any entertainment, lottery or art union, any building, private residence, boat or vehicle, or any charitable or other institution'.

Even *Anzac biscuits* are protected by law. Well, not so much the biscuits as their name. And, by the way, *Anzac* is no longer an acronym – it is now officially a word: that means the 'A' is upper case and the rest of the letters should be lower case.

In *Digger Dialects* Dowling tells us that during World War I *Anzac* had two other meanings: as the name of the area on the Gallipoli peninsula occupied by the A.I.F and the N.Z.E.F. (New Zealand Expeditionary Force); and as a sarcastic nickname for a military policeman.

Once the word *Anzac* had been born it, in turn, became part of a number of other expressions. Dowling says that an *Anzac button* was a nail used in place of a trouser button; *Anzac soup* was shell-hole water polluted by a corpse (reflecting the grim humour of soldiers in combat); *Anzac stew* was army food that (according to legend) consisted of an urn of hot water and one bacon rind; and an *Anzac wafer* was the hard biscuit supplied to the AIF in place of bread (Dowling comments: 'One of the most durable materials used in the war').

Back home the wives, girlfriends and mums of the Australian soldiers started cooking sweet Anzac biscuits (a different version to the Army biscuit) to ship over to their blokes. They were originally called soldiers' biscuits, but after the landing on Gallipoli they were given their present name. To this day Anzac biscuits remain one of Australia's national foods. And just in case you've missed out on this culinary delight, here's a recipe (this one is from the Australian War Memorial):

Ingredients

1 cup each of plain flour, sugar, rolled oats and coconut

4 oz butter

1 tablespoon golden syrup

2 tablespoons boiling water

1 teaspoon carbonate of soda (add a little more water if mixture is too dry)

Method

1. Grease biscuit tray and preheat oven to 180° C.

2. Combine dry ingredients.

3. Melt together butter and golden syrup. Combine water and soda, add to butter mixture.

4. Mix butter mixture and dry ingredients.

5. Drop teaspoons of mixture onto tray allowing room for spreading.

6. Bake for 10–15 minutes or until golden. Allow to cool on tray for a few minutes before transferring to cooling racks

And why are there no eggs? Because, apparently, most poultry farmers had joined up so eggs were scarce. Golden syrup took the place of eggs as the binding agent.

Then, from 1916, April 25 was named as Anzac Day. In that first year it was marked by a wide variety of ceremonies and services in Australia, a march through London, and a sports day in the Australian camp in Egypt. In London, over 2000 Australian and New Zealand troops marched through the streets of the city. A London newspaper headline dubbed them 'The Knights of Gallipoli'.

Marches were held all over Australia in 1916. Wounded

soldiers from Gallipoli attended the Sydney march in convoys of cars, attended by nurses. For the remaining years of the First World War, Anzac Day was used as an occasion for patriotic rallies and recruiting campaigns, and parades of serving members of the AIF were held in most cities.

During the 1920s, Anzac Day became established as a national day of commemoration for the more than 60 000 Australians who died during the Great War. The first year in which all the states observed some form of public holiday together on 25 April was 1927.

By the mid-1930s all the rituals now associated with the day (dawn services, marches, reunions, and two-up games) were firmly established as part of Anzac Day culture.

With the coming of the Second World War, Anzac Day became a day on which to commemorate the lives of Australians lost in that war as well, and in subsequent years its meaning has been further broadened to include Australians killed in all the military operations in which the nation has been involved.

Arguably, 25 April, Anzac Day, is Australia's most significant national day.

Another word that took on a permanent and nationally significant meaning during the First World War is *digger*. As we've already noticed, this first appeared as an Aussie word during the gold rushes but it was on the battlefields of 1914–18 that *digger* was given a new lease of life and a wider meaning.

In 1918 the Australian soldiers' magazine *Aussie* defined a *digger* as 'a friend, a pal, or comrade, synonymous with cobbers'. And on the origin of the word the same magazine wrote: 'It came to France when the sandgropers gave up digging on the goldfields of W.A. and carried on with it on the battlefields'.

By way of explanation, *sandgroper* has been a nickname for the residents of Western Australia since 1896 (to *sand-grope* means 'to walk in soft sand' and is, presumably, the source of the nickname).

To this day in Australia a false or unreliable rumour is a *furphy*. The earliest recorded use is 1915, and comes from the diggers of the First World War. You've already encountered in chapter 1 the story of the firm of Joe Furphy & Sons of Shepparton, makers of the army water-carts where diggers gathered and gossiped. The name Furphy was prominently displayed on the back of each cart, and became the name for the unreliable information exchanged there, hence the slang term for (especially unreliable) gossip.

And each Furphy water-cart had the following words of wisdom on the side: 'Good, better, best: never let it rest, until your good is better – and your better best'. That's the kind of motto our grandparents lived by (and it didn't do them any harm, either). WH Dowling also records the expression *furphy king*, meaning 'a retailer of rumours.'

As an aside showing how such word formation works, that other (non-Aussie) slang word for gossip, *scuttlebutt*, was born in exactly same way. *Scuttlebutt* turned up in the era when the great sailing ships crossed the oceans of the world (providing Australia, in those days, with its only link to the European culture that had given birth to the nation). The *scuttle* on a sailing ship was a square or rectangular opening, a bit smaller than a proper hatchway. The scuttle was often close to the mainmast. And just next to the scuttle was a *butt* – that being an old name for a water cask. This place where the crew went for a drink was the *scuttlebutt* – and it was the place where they exchanged gossip. Thus *furphy* and *scuttlebutt* not only have almost identical meanings, they were born in almost exactly the same way.

In 1918 Allied forces under the command of General Allenby defeated the Ottoman army in Palestine and Syria, and on 30 October the Ottoman Empire signed an armistice. As the war in Europe staggered on, Germany teetered on the edge of collapse, with the German people facing starvation because of a British naval blockade. On the morning of 11 November 1918, the Germans accepted the armistice terms demanded by the Allies. The war was over.

Anzac troops began the slow journey home, and the return to civilian life. As they did so, they were to discover that Aussie English had not been standing still on the home front either.

WORD LIST

Obviously in this chapter I have discussed only three of the words that appeared during the First World War – because I wanted to discuss each of them at some length. There were, of course, many more. And below is a selection of words and phrases – a good many of which were coined well before the war, but it was World War I that put them into wider circulation, and it's that widespread usage that WH Dowling captured in his book. Some were American in origin, and were discovered and borrowed by Aussie English only when Australian and American troops rubbed shoulders.

'ALF A MO a small moustache (a play on the expression 'half a moment'; I remember my father calling such a facial decoration 'a cricket match – eleven hairs on each side').

BACK CHAT (1) an impertinent bandying of words; (2) to answer back.

BAGS plenty, a large number.

BINGE a drunken orgy.

BIRD (1) a person; (2) a girl; (3) a military prisoner.

BLOOD'S WORTH BOTTLING A phrase expressive of admiration. (Dowling is the first to record this expression which follows closely, in time, the development of safe blood transfusions in 1901 with the discovery of human blood groups. The First World War may have seen the first contact many had with blood transfusion, hence the source of the expression.)

BLOTTO inebriated.

BRASS HAT an officer of superior rank.

BREEZE-UP fear.

BUCKSHEE free, gratuitous (from the Arabic *bakshish*).

BUNK abscond, or 'do a bunk'.

C'EST LA GUERRE 'It's the war'; a phrase used on any and every occasion.

CHAI tea.

CHAT to tell a person something.

COFFIN NAIL cigarette.

CUSHY soft, easy or safe (e.g. a cushy job at the base).

DOLL UP to ornament.

DOUGH money.

DUCK'S BREAKFAST a drink of water and a wash (a frequent repast on the front line).

DUG IN a safe or comfortable position.

FANGS 'to put in the fangs' – to demand money, etc.

FILL AN EYE to punch in the eye.

FLAT SPIN to be in difficulties.

FLOG, TO to worry.

FLY (TO GIVE IT A) to make an attempt.

GIGGLE HOUSE lunatic asylum.

GO CROOK become angry or abusive.

GO TO THE PACK deteriorate (probably a variation on 'go to the dogs').

GUTSER a disappointment; a misfortune; *to come a gutser* to suffer a reversal of fortune.

IT'S A NICE DAY FOR IT! sardonic phrase applied to anything unpleasant; e.g. an attack which is likely to be costly.

LEAD-SWINGER a person who schemes with the object of avoiding duty in dangerous areas; a malingerer.

MEAT-HOOK arm.

NAIL-SCISSORS the crossed sword and baton worn as a badge of rank by a general.

NIP to cadge (or 'put in the nips').

NOSE-BLEEDS red tabs worn by staff officers.

NUT 'nut it out' – think it out.

OVER THE ODDS unconscionable.

PONG stink.

PORT-HOLES IN YOUR COFFIN (to want) to be hard to please.

POZZIE position; place; dugout; home.

POT, TO to shoot.

PUSH IN intrude.

RAT-AND-FOWL Australian shilling (the shilling coin featured the Australian coat of arms showing a kangaroo and an emu).

RISSOLE KING army cook.

SHRAPNEL pork and beans.

SNIFTER excellent.

SOUVENIR, TO to steal, find, capture, etc.

STONKER, TO to exterminate; kill; strike out.

THIEVING IRONS hands.

TOO RIGHT certainly. (The linguists say this is the earliest recorded occurrence of this phrase, which in the following decades became so common in Aussie English as to be almost a verbal tic.)

TREACLE-MINER a man who boasts of his wealth or his position in private life.

TURN SOUR become angry.

TURN-UP a lucky event (origin of the still current expression 'that's a turn-up for the books').

12

THE HOME FRONT

Aussie English was born into a very blokey atmosphere. At its birth the convict colony must have resembled the changing rooms at a rugby match – composed of equal parts of sweat, bravado and excuses for what went wrong after that second tackle – for in those early days men vastly outnumbered women.

Among the early settlers on the sprawling sheep and cattle runs of the bush there were also many more men than women. There were women on the gold diggings – but, once again, they were outnumbered. This blokiness was reinforced by the experience of war – of soldiers cut off from their womenfolk as they sadly whistled 'Keep the Home Fires Burning'.

But despite all this blokiness there were, of course, always women around. We've already noticed that 180 of the 717 convicts on the First Fleet were women. Among their descendants were currency lasses as well as currency lads. And from the beginning the women were doing what they always do – shaking their heads in sheer disbelief at the boofiness of their blokes while getting on with the job of keeping the place going. They had babies and they made homes for their families.

In his classic short story 'The Drover's Wife', Henry Lawson painted an unforgettable picture of their courage and their iron nerve. These were the brave women who 'wouldn't say die till a dead horse kicked them'. And all the while – as they dressed and fed their families and killed the occasional snake (see 'The Drover's Wife' for details) – they had their own fun with Aussie English.

While the blokes were off droving a massive mob of cattle down the Canning Stock Route (or digging for gold or fighting in the trenches), mum and the kids were back home coining the sort of expressions that give us a glimpse of private life – of what was going on behind the cafe curtains on the kitchen window.

Which brings us to the story of Nancy Keesing – born in Sydney in 1923 into a world recovering from the Great War and a society marked by returned soldiers back in civvies, back with their women and kids, and trying to reconstruct the lives they had before 'the big stoush'.

Nancy Keesing's parents sent her first to SCEGGS (the Sydney Church of England Girls' Grammar School) and then to Frensham School for her education. From there she went on to Sydney University and to a lifetime as a writer immersed in the rich world of language – and especially of Aussie English. She connected, in a special way, with the history of our language in 1952 when she went to work at *The Bulletin* and the poet Douglas Stewart became her early mentor.

In the years that followed she wrote novels, poetry and memoirs. With Douglas Stewart she compiled the landmark anthology *Old Bush Songs* (a vastly expanded revision of Banjo Paterson's book of the same name). And by the time she came to write *Lily on the Dustbin* she was in her late fifties and had a lifetime of listening to the domestic use of Aussie English with her sharp poet's ear.

Keesing described *Lily on the Dustbin* as a record of the 'slang of Australian women and families'. Throughout the book she refers to this branch of Aussie English as either 'Sheilaspeak' or 'Familyspeak'.

In writing her book she relied, she tells us, more on oral sources than printed ones because 'for some reason most Australian novelists – men as well as women – between 1920 and 1970 chose not to write about kids, kitchens and kindergartens or, when they did, chose to select certain colloquial terms and reject a whole range of others'. So she drew on her own memories, the memories of her friends and family, and the memories of hundreds of women who called her on radio open-line shows to share the slang of their domestic childhoods.

I have tried the same exercise on radio, and I've been flooded with grandmas calling to tell me what *their* grandmas said many decades earlier. They joyously remembered being told at night to settle down and go to sleep because 'it won't be this in the morning!' Then if the kids obeyed their instructions and snuggled down, they might be told they were 'as snug as a bug in a rug' – an expression mum might have picked up from Paterson's much-loved 'A Bush Christening'. If one of the kids overslept the next morning they were likely to be roused with the words 'You've missed the best part of the day' (spoken loudly, and at close range).

Less joyously, my open-line callers remembered the domestic drudgery of those pre-electronic gadgetry days.

> **copper** in Familyspeak not a policeman, but a large heated copper tub in which clothes were boiled before washing machines became widely available.

Originally the *copper* (which is how one always spoke of that big lump of a thing in the corner of the laundry) was heated by a wood fire. My mother still used a copper in the very early years of my childhood, but by then it had a gas ring underneath it for heating. I can still remember her stirring the clothes in the bubbling copper with a big wooden stick and pulling them out one by one (with the same stick) and cranking them through a hand-wringer to squeeze out most of the water. To complete their drying the clothes were hung out on the clothesline.

In those days it was a straight clothesline, quite possibly held up in its sagging middle by a *clothes prop* – a long, reasonably straight sapling or pole with a Y-shape at the top end to hook up the line heavy with wet clothes. This, however, disappeared in the years following World War II to be replaced by the:

Hills Hoist a height-adjustable, rotary clothes line manufactured by Adelaide inventor Lance Hill starting in 1945. It gradually became the most prominent item in most Aussie backyards.

It was equalled in its ubiquity only by the ...

barbie Aussie for barbecue or for the meal cooked on the barbecue. The original word seems to be of Spanish origin, and began as the name for a framework of sticks set upon posts. Interestingly, it was first recorded (with this original meaning) by William Dampier in 1697. Dampier (1651–1715) was the first Englishman to explore parts of what is today Australia. It would be nice to think he was also the first bloke to cook a barbecue on these shores, but in his day the word hadn't yet shifted to mean a metal framework with a fire underneath to nicely char the sausages. The barbie form of the word was first recorded in Australia in 1976.

But let's get back inside the house and listen to what the mums are saying to their kids. If the children are underfoot and annoying they are likely to be told to 'Pretend you're a tap and run!' or 'Pretend you're an egg and beat it!'. If the household teenager has a messy room they might to be told 'This looks like it was stirred with a stick' or 'This looks like a chook run on Christmas Day with all the chooks drunk!'.

In the kitchen, at washing-up time, if the kids were playing at flicking each other with teatowels instead of getting on with the job they were likely to be told 'Those dishes won't dry themselves, you know'.

Also in the kitchen, if mum lost track of the time (while she was 'having a natter with her next door') and the scones were overcooked, the kids might call them 'possum knockers' (good only for throwing at possums on low branches).

The names of daily meals prepared in that kitchen appear to have changed over the years. The midday meal was once called 'dinner' and the main evening meal was 'tea'. This usage seems to have vanished now, replaced by the rather more mundane 'lunch' and 'dinner'.

Turning from the kitchen to the dining room – if the kids were very hungry they might wolf down a meal so fast that mum would say 'I'll bet that didn't touch the sides on the way down'. Mind you, if mum saw you eating too fast she'd tell you there was no rush: 'If there's a fire they'll ring the bell'. This was a warning to slow down and eat properly.

For lunch the children might be given a Vegemite sandwich, or perhaps Vegemite between two Vita-Weat biscuits. The real pleasure in this latter snack was that you could squeeze the Vita-Weats together and see wiggly worms of black Vegemite emerge from the holes. You licked off the worms before eating the biscuits.

If a child was made to wear a garment handed down from an older sibling, they might be told that it 'fits all over and touches nowhere' (not intended as a flattering fashion statement).

Then if life was getting a bit too much, mum might decide that what she needed was a Bex or, possibly, 'a cup of tea, a Bex and a good lie down'. Bex was the brand name of a well-known headache powder made by Beckers. They were advertised on radio for many years with the almost chanted slogan of 'B-E-X … Bex is better!'

The three ingredients in Bex, and other similar headache powders, like Vincent's APC, were aspirin, phenacetin and caffeine, and were promised to bring 'quick three-way relief'. Unfortunately it was later discovered that phenacetin could cause kidney damage and it was withdrawn from use in 1983.

What produced the headache in the first place? Well, possibly an endlessly chattering child. The child would be told they could 'talk the leg off a table' or 'off an iron pot'. The version I remember from my own childhood was 'you could talk the hind leg off a donkey' (why the animal's forelegs were regarded as safe I have no idea).

Or the child might be told to stop hanging around the house and 'go and play in the yard'. Outside, at least in the summer months, the kids might collect cicadas, snatching them off a low branch and putting them into an old cardboard shoebox. But they were not called cicadas in those days – they were always and only called locusts. They were named for their colour schemes. The most common of them were the 'green grocers'. Much rarer were the 'floury baker' and the 'black prince.'

This brings us to that most distinctive of all Aussie domestic words, that bit of land between the back door of the house and the back fence:

> **backyard** defined by the *Australian National Dictionary* as 'an enclosure, usually including a garden in which fruit and vegetables are grown at the back of a house'. The word is first recorded here by Watkin Tench in 1793. He was a British marine officer who travelled to Australia on the First Fleet, and who recorded his experiences in the books *Narrative of the Expedition to Botany Bay* and *Complete Account of the Settlement at Port Jackson.*

So *backyard* appears to have been there at the birth of Aussie English. It clearly began life as a straight descriptive – a 'yard' that was at the 'back'. And it's recorded as such in the United States in 1659 – long before our distinctive dialect of English was born. Nevertheless I'm claiming it as ours because of its universal existence in the 'quarter-acre block' of the Australian suburb, and the frequency of its use in conversational Aussie.

For example, it was the place where generations of Aussie kids played:

> **backyard cricket** a game played between sides of uneven numbers, using a box as the stumps, a cricket bat and any available ball (an old tennis ball would do) and featuring the famous rule 'six and out' to cover any ball hit over the fence into next door's place (you scored your six but you lost your wicket).

Sadly, with the rise of the McMansion with its back wall only a metre or so from the back fence, and the drift towards apartment living, this great Aussie growing-up space – and the games played over its tangle of paspalum and buffalo grass – may be disappearing.

Which brings us to the contribution Aussie kids have made (and continue to make) to Aussie English – and to the story of June Factor, the collector of their lively and wonderful slang.

Factor is one of those impossibly brainy people who combines rigorous academic research with a sense of humour and an eye (and ear) for what ordinary people are up to. This has generated her book about Aussie kids' folklore, *Captain Cook*

Chased a Chook, and her collections of those sayings for the kids themselves: *Far Out, Brussel Sprout!*, *All Right, Vegemite!*, *Unreal, Banana Peel!*, *Real Keen, Baked Bean!*, *Roll Over, Pavlova!* and *Okey Dokey, Karaoke!*

Factor's book *Kidspeak: A Dictionary of Australian Children's Words, Expressions and Games* appeared in 2000 – an impressive collection. She shows us that Aussie kids are continuing to display the verbal inventiveness of the generations of Aussies who've been playing around with our language from the moment of its birth (a fact we'll return to in our last chapter). For example:

> **braceface** a person wearing dental braces, usually used as an insult.

That's not an expression that was around when I was a kid, but I can easily imagine one child calling out to another across the school playground, 'Hey! Braceface, are you in this game or not?'

> **get your bra in a twist (don't)** don't overreact [update on 'don't get your knickers in a knot'].

But among this ongoing invention, it's nice to discover that some of the old slang I knew as a child still survives, such as:

> **brinnie** a small stone, especially one used by small boys to throw at other small boys in the rough and tumble of schoolyard battles (also spelled 'brinny').

Factor makes the point that for small children words and language start off in life as something to play with – from 'this little piggy went to market ...' onwards. And playing with words is what Aussie English is good at.

For their mothers, on the other hand, language is often what conveys the family's traditions of good behaviour to the children. (If we started acting up in a department store Mum would rebuke us by saying 'Remember you're out!' – the implication being that we should save our silly stuff for when we were at home.) But whether playing with words or neatly summarising the family's standards and traditions, Aussie English is at its most comfortable when it's at home.

Well, we've now chased Aussie English through every room of the house (and out into the backyard, off to school and back home again) and we've rather got ahead of ourselves. This story of domestic talk started when the boys came home from the First World War. It continued through the 1920s and 30s and on into later decades.

So now we need to step back into our timeline, back into the history of our language, with the 1930s drawing to a close, and Aussie English about to slip off its civvies, slip into a uniform, and march off to war once more.

WORD LIST

Nancy Keesing and June Factor have collected many examples of Aussie English from the kitchens, verandahs and backyards of Aussie homes in their admirable books. I have collected other examples from callers to my radio open-line show over the years. The following is a small selection.

BADGER! an expression uttered by schoolboys after breaking wind. It's followed quickly by a whistling noise. This ritual prevents other schoolboys from pummelling the perpetrator for his antisocial offence.

BAR 1 (1) an exclamation used to gain a respite from the rules during a children's game; (2) a designated place where such safety is found during a game. From *barley*, which has been used in this way by children (reports Factor) since the fourteenth century (possibly originally from the French *parlez*, in English 'parley' – a place of truce, safe quarters). There is some evidence that this outcry used in children's play continued in Australia after it had died out in Britain.

BAR 2 (1) to carry a second person on a horse, bicycle or motorcycle; (2) to ride as a secondary passenger.

BORN IN A TENT? question put to someone who comes through a door and leaves it open.

CHARLIE'S MOVING THE FURNITURE said to a small child to account for a loud crash of thunder.

CHASINGS a schoolyard game that involves chasing and catching (sometimes called 'chasey').

CHUCK A WOBBLY have a temper tantrum.

CUNNING AS A DUNNY RAT, AS a smooth operator.

DADDY LONGLEGS child's name for a small, spindly spider common in Australian homes.

DAG, DAGGY a person who is completely unstylish, or totally lacking in any social skills or graces. Originally a *dag* was a clump of dried faeces matted in the wool around the rear end of a sheep.

DOG'S DISEASE any one of the following: (1) a bad head cold; (2) the flu; (3) gastroenteritis.

DUCHESS either: (1) a dressing table; or (2) a doily set – consisting of one longer doily and two smaller ones – to go on a dressing table.

DUDS sometimes clothing in general, sometimes only referring to underwear.

DUFFER term of affection for a small child who's had an accident or made a mistake (sometimes in the form of 'you're a silly duffer').

DUNNY BUDGIE a large blowfly.

EARLY MARK being let out of school early.

FLAKE OUT collapse, lie down.

FLY CEMETERY a fruit slice.

FULL (NO THANKS, I'M) rejecting a second helping (indicating one has eaten an elegant sufficiency).

FULL AS A GOOG variation on the above, the 'goog' part referring to a 'googy egg' (children's slang for an egg) since eggs are completely full to their shell (see below).

GARBAGE GUTS a greedy person.

GOOGY EGG (OR GOOG FOR SHORT) childish name for an egg. Its source has puzzled me for years. The only suggestion I've ever come across is that each of the two Os in the middle resemble the shape of an egg. But that still doesn't explain the rest of the word.

HIT AND GIGGLE housewives' tennis.

IT WON'T BE THIS IN THE MORNING warning given to small children reluctant to go to bed.

LICKETTY SPLIT instruction to a child to do something quickly.

LILY ON THE DUSTBIN either: (1) a woman who is overdressed for a social occasion, or (2) a woman left languishing and alone at a social event.

LIPPIE lipstick.

MAGPIE a person who is an obsessive collector of trifles.

MUTTON DRESSED AS LAMB a woman wearing clothes inappropriately young for her age.

PULL YOUR SOCKS UP! do better, or, at least, make an effort.

RAT'S COFFIN meat pie.

ROUGH AS BAGS a comment on a person's social skills.

RUN UP what a woman does to a piece of material to turn it into a dress; she 'runs up a dress'.

SHUT MOUTH CATCHES NO FLIES (REMEMBER A) a warning not to repeat family gossip outside the home.

SLOW AS A WET WEEK (YOU'RE AS) said to a small child who's dawdling.

SNOT BAR a vanilla slice.

SO'S CHRISTMAS! reply to a slow child who shouts 'I'm coming!'.

SPEND A PENNY go to the dunny (women's toilets, but not men's, once had locked cubicles that could be opened only by inserting a penny coin in the slot).

STEP-INS suspender belt.

TICKETS ON YOURSELF (DON'T HAVE) don't boast.

TOUGHEN UP BUTTERCUP encouragement from a wife to her husband when he comes down with a bad dose of 'man flu'.

TWO HAIRS PAST A FRECKLE the reply you give when asked the time if you're not wearing a wristwatch.

WASH UP AS FAR AS POSSIBLE, THEN DOWN AS FAR AS POSSIBLE, THEN WASH WHAT'S POSSIBLE wash your face before you wash your feet (and wash what's in between last of all).

WISH IN ONE HAND AND SPIT IN THE OTHER, SEE WHICH FILLS UP FIRST response to a child who expresses a wish the family can't afford.

13

WORDS AT WAR (AGAIN!)

The 1930s reminded Aussies that you didn't have to be in the army to be doing it tough. The Great Depression hit ordinary working families like a slap in the eye with a wet sock. As unemployment soared and hearts sank, Aussie families carried on as they always did – making do: living in shanties, clearing bits of land to grow vegetables, trapping rabbits, and doing any bits of work that might pay a shilling. Their struggle ended not with a return to prosperity, but with a return to the battlefront.

World War II began on radio. Tension had been building across Europe as Hitler became steadily more aggressive. Having absorbed Austria and other territories on the borders of Germany, on 1 September 1939 Hitler invaded Poland.

Two days later Britons huddled around their radios to hear their Prime Minister, Neville Chamberlain, say: 'I am speaking to you from the Cabinet Room of 10 Downing Street. This morning the British Ambassador in Berlin handed the German government a final note, stating that unless we heard from them – by 11 o'clock – that they were prepared at once to withdraw their troops from Poland, a state of war would exist between us. I have to tell you now that no such undertaking has been received and that, consequently, this country is at war with Germany.'

At 9:15 that night, Australians gathered around their crackling radio sets to hear Prime Minister Robert Menzies pronounce these solemn words: 'Fellow Australians, it is my melancholy duty to inform you officially that, in consequence of the persistence of Germany in her invasion of Poland, Great Britain has declared war upon her, and that, as a result, Australia is also at war.'

Those words, from those leaders, cast the pattern that was to shape the next six years. And along with the blood and the bullets it was to be a conflict marked, and shaped, by words. There were, for example, these famous words from Franklin D Roosevelt in his radio broadcast following the Japanese bombing of Pearl Harbor, in which he described 'yesterday, December 7, 1941' as 'a date that will live in infamy'.

And the whole world, not just Britain and the British Commonwealth, was gripped and moved by the powerful words rumbled out by Winston Churchill in his wartime radio broadcasts:

> I have nothing to offer but blood, toil, tears and sweat.

We shall fight on the beaches, we shall fight on the landing grounds, we shall fight in the fields and in the streets, we shall fight in the hills; we shall never surrender.

Let us therefore brace ourselves to our duty, and so bear ourselves that, if the British Commonwealth and its Empire lasts for a thousand years, men will still say, 'This was their finest hour'.

And of all the words employed in this worldwide 'war waged with words', the most cheerful and the most cheeky were coined by Aussies.

For Australians the Second World War turned out to be a very different experience from the First. It was no less destructive, and its horrors and atrocities were no less, but it came much closer to home. On 15 September 1939, Prime Minister Menzies announced the formation of the 2nd AIF (Australian Imperial Force). This was to be an expeditionary force of (to begin with) 20 000 men.

For Aussies the Second World War was at the start fought mainly in North Africa against the Italians and the Germans. The conflict included the heroism of the famous 'rats of Tobruk' (the 14 000 Australian soldiers besieged for 240 days in the Libyan port city of Tobruk by the might of Rommel's 'desert army', the Deutsches Afrika Corps).

But from the bombing of Pearl Harbor in December 1941 the Australian focus switched to the war against Japan in the Pacific. This included the slogging jungle battle along the Kokoda Track in Papua New Guinea, and naval conflicts such as the Battle of the Coral Sea.

It also brought the war to Australia's shores with Japanese

midget submarines entering Sydney Harbour in May 1942 with the intention of attacking Allied warships. One of the submarines ran aground harmlessly, but the other hit the breakwater against which HMAS *Kuttabul* and a Dutch submarine were moored. The explosion broke *Kuttabul* in two and sank her, with the loss of nineteen lives.

Even before then, in February of that year, Japanese aircraft attacked the city of Darwin, and the ships in Darwin harbour. This was the beginning of almost one hundred air raids against northern Australia during 1942–43. Also in February 1942, Singapore fell to the rapidly advancing Japanese Army. More than 22 000 *Australians* became prisoners of war of the Japanese in South-east Asia. By the end of the war a total of 39 366 Australians had died. Many more had been wounded or affected by the impact of the war.

And there is, of course, something about warfare, and the way society is organised in war time, that causes language to explode in new directions and new ways. I follow the example of the professor of communications who famously said: 'Never repeat for emphasis. I'll say that again – never repeat for emphasis'. So I'll repeat what I said about the First World War: Exactly why wartime produces such rapid change in language is not certain, but it has something to do with so many people being thrust together, from different walks of life, dealing with unusual circumstances. In those conditions new words and phrases are coined rapidly, some of which become permanent parts of the language after the conflict ends.

And some of the expressions born in the Second World War continued to live in civilian life in the years that followed. For example:

bodger fake or false or worthless or badly done. First recorded in the *Biscuit Bomber Weekly*, the magazine of the 1st Australian Air Maintenance Company in 1945.

In the peacetime years that followed this gave us *bodgie* – most commonly used to describe anything that's worthless, either because it's a fake, or because it's broken. So 'bodgie number plates' are fakes, and a job that's 'a bit bodgie' is one that's not done well. Behind the word *bodger* is the very old English word *bodge*, meaning 'a botched piece of work' (in fact *bodge* and *botch* seem originally to have been the same word).

In the 1950s, however, *bodgie* briefly had another meaning. Then a *bodgie* was a young Australian male who conformed to certain fashions in dress and loutish or rowdy behaviour. His female counterpart was a *widgie*. The *bodgie*'s trademarks were greasy hair and tight jeans. This use of the word seems to go back to the notion of *bodgie* as 'fake' – in this case they were seen as being fake Americans, or 'half-baked Yanks', or *bodgies*.

As a child I can remember using other wartime coinages, such as:

lolly water soft drink, the soldier's last resort when something stronger is not available. My memory is of my uncles using this to describe what we kids called 'soft drinks'.

no-hoper a person who is a useless waste of space. Perhaps this usage is fading a little now, but it remained common for decades after the end of the war.

However, still common is the word used when I was in high school as an alternative to 'flaking out', namely:

crash collapse in sleep, either after a heavy bout of work of fighting, or after a heavy drinking session.

Nowadays I suspect only older Aussies would tell you they are slightly less than gruntled and generally unhappy with things by saying that they are:

brassed-off disgruntled, grumpy, or, possibly completely fed up! Perhaps originally from the Navy, where polishing the ship's brass was an unwelcome duty.

Mind you, not all of the Aussie language of the Second World War was brand new. There are some earlier expressions that belong in this chapter because they were put into much wider circulation by the social currents of the conflict. For instance, the following name for something you have no name for may have been around (possibly as *doofer*) in the 1930s. But it was during the war years it became widespread, and settled into its familiar form:

doover a thing, a doodad, a thingummyjig – sometimes in the form **dooverlackie**, referring to any gadget or thing for which you don't have a proper name. *Doover* is one of those words that is used when you can't remember (or don't know) the proper name for something. According to one yarn, *doover* was also slang for the bed pans used in military hospitals – and the bloke who had to empty the bed pans was the *dooverlackie* (*lackey* being a very old word for a servant). It's a good story … it might even be true. The *Australian National Dictionary* suggests *doover* may come from the Yiddish word *davar*, meaning 'a word or thing'.

The word *blue* had been a distinctively Aussie word from the late nineteenth century when it was commonly used to mean either a swag or a person with red hair. During the war years it took on two new meanings:

> **blue** (1) a fight or a battle. In 1943 war correspondent Allan Dawes wrote 'I heard the blue [meaning the battle] was still on'; (2) a mistake. Linguist Amanda Laugesen suggests this is an abbreviation of the British slang term *bloomer*, meaning 'a very great mistake'. The abbreviation, however, comes from Aussies and comes from the Second World War.

Aussie English is very fond of expressions to describe someone as 'two bob short of a quid'; one of the most distinctive of these was born in the 1920s but spread its wings and became a national linguistic treasure during World War II:

> **drongo** a bit of an idiot, a no-hoper. The story goes that there was a racehorse named Drongo (running between 1923–25). This horse, supposedly, always ran last (or near to last). Cartoonist Sammy Wells, then of the Melbourne *Herald*, apparently adopted Drongo as a character in his political and sporting cartoons. In these cartoons Drongo was the no-hoper in every situation. That's the story that's told.

However, the earliest citation for the word *drongo* is from the Melbourne *Argus* of 1924, and says (quote): 'Drongo is sure to be a very hard horse to beat. He is improving with every run.' But that doesn't sound like a horse that consistently ran last (or near to last). Furthermore, there was a bird called a *drongo*

— and, just possibly, the insult *you drongo* originally meant 'you birdbrain'. Or perhaps both the bird *and* the racehorse played a part in the adoption of *drongo* into Aussie English. Whichever it was, it was the gathering of men from across Australia in barracks that spread the term far and wide.

Then on 6 June 1944, tens of thousands of Allied troops stormed up the beaches of Normandy into the teeth of the German guns. The liberation of conquered Europe had begun. Months of hard fighting followed. On 30 April 1945 Adolf Hitler committed suicide in his bunker in Berlin. As German resistance collapsed across all the European battlefronts, 9 May 1945 was declared to be VE Day ('Victory in Europe' Day).

In the Pacific, Japan fought on until on 6 August 1945 the United States dropped an atomic bomb on Hiroshima. Three days later another was dropped on Nagasaki. Three months after the liberation of Europe, 15 August 1945 was declared to be VP Day ('Victory in the Pacific' Day). The gates of the POW camps were thrown open and the prisoners were freed. And, across the Pacific and around the world, Australian service personnel looked forward to being *demobbed* ('demobilised') and getting back to their homes and their families.

So for the second time in the span of a single lifetime Aussie English was demobbed and back home again. But it came back to discover that it was being noticed and recorded more carefully, and with more interest and delight, than ever before.

WORD LIST

The definitive book on Australian wartime slang is *Diggerspeak: The language of Australians at war* by Amanda Laugesen (2005).

However, there are numerous other glossaries and word lists. For example, Rohan Rivett includes a glossary at the end of his book about the Australian POW experience in the Pacific, *Behind Bamboo*; Lawson Glossop did the same with his novel about the North Africa campaign, *We Were the Rats*. AG Mitchell wrote a number of articles about military slang during the war years; and the Australian National War Memorial has a collection of data on the subject. The following is a select list of some of the more colourful items collated from these resources.

ACK-WILLY absent without leave (from the signal code for 'A' and 'W').

BARDIA BILL a heavy artillery gun that bombarded Tobruk during the 1941 siege. (From the name of a town in north-eastern Libya defended by the Italians. The first Australian action in North Africa, in January 1941, was the capture of Bardia.)

BASH-ARTIST a guard in a POW camp who beat up prisoners.

BEAUEY a Bristol Beaufighter, a long-range heavy fighter aircraft. The Brits shortened this to 'Beau' and the Australians added the distinctive 'Y' ending found so often in Aussie English.

BISCUIT BOMBER an aircraft that dropped food and other supplies to troops in remote parts of New Guinea.

BLITZ BUGGY *Blitz* is a German word meaning 'lightning'. It was used by the Germans in the term *Blitzkrieg* to describe their 'lightning strike' style of attack. It was picked up by English language users to describe the bombing of London as the 'blitz on Britain'. From there the use of the word spread. Early in the war ambulances were called *blitz buggies*, but later the label was applied any fast vehicle (one that 'moved like lightning'), and was used by Aussie soldiers especially for an open truck, such as a troop carrier.

BLUE ORCHID a member of the Royal Australian Air Force (from the RAAF's blue uniforms – used in a mocking sense by the army and the navy).

BOMB-HAPPY slightly off one's rocker because of the constant rain of enemy bombs.

BULLO unreliable information, or complete fantasy. Aussies had been using *bull* and *bull dust* as labels for nonsense for some time. During the war the typical Aussie 'O' ending was added.

CIVVY STREET civilian life; what servicemen (and women) were longing to get back to just as soon as the 'big blue' was over.

DINGER the backside. In his 1943 book *Target Area* John Binning wrote: 'War consists of one hour of action and excitement followed by days of *dinger* drill' [sitting about waiting].

DIT (TO SPIN A) to spin a yarn – chiefly a naval term.

DON R a dispatch rider (from the signal code for the letter D).

DONGA a temporary shelter, used as early as 1900 for any makeshift dwelling; widely used by soldiers sent to defend Australia's northern shoreline from possible Japanese invasion.

DOOVER HOLE a trench or dugout (from *doover* – see above).

DRAW THE CROW draw the short straw, get stuck with the worst end of the deal.

DROP-SHORTS artillery term for shells that drop short of their target.

DUCK name given to a type of Japanese warplane (according to one war correspondent they were a kind of cumbersome seaplane).

EARBASH to talk incessantly.

EARBASHER one who does this.

EYETIE derogatory term for an Italian. Although this was known in the First World War, it was during the North Africa campaign in the Second that it became widespread.

FLAK-HAPPY a pilot who takes careless risks, perhaps sent slightly barmy by the amount of anti-aircraft fire he has come under.

FLYING COFFIN an aircraft at risk of crashing or being shot down, especially applied to aircraft that were old or not particularly airworthy.

FOO an RAAF term for the cause of all problems; sometimes an expletive, sometimes referring to a person (perhaps an imaginary person) who has got everything wrong; possibly an abbreviation of *fubar* (pronounced 'foobar'); see below.

FUBAR 'fouled up beyond all recognition' (although occasionally soldiers, sailors and airmen have been known to substitute another F-word for 'fouled').

FUZZY WUZZY a native of New Guinea.

FUZZY WUZZY ANGEL a native of New Guinea acting as a stretcher bearer for wounded Australian troops.

GEN information (as in 'Have you got the *gen*?'), pronounced with a soft G – sometimes unreliable information, camp gossip.

GIGGLE SUIT army fatigues, often ill-fitting, and regarded as generally comical in appearance

GLAMOUR dress uniform, a vast improvement over the *giggle suit*.

GOLDFISH tinned fish.

GOONSKIN another name for *giggle suit*. AG Mitchell thought the expression came from a character in the *Popeye* comic strip.

GRIFF reliable information, more reliable than *gen*.

HOMER a wound bad enough to guarantee you'll be sent home (back to Australia).

JERRY German soldier; 'Fritz' and 'Hun' were more common in the First World War, 'Jerry' in the Second.

JUNGLE-HAPPY like *bomb-happy* and *flak-happy*, this described someone who'd gone slightly crazy, in this case from spending too much time in the jungle.

LADY BLAMEY a drinking glass used by soldiers, made out of an empty bottle. It's claimed that it was the wife of

General Sir Thomas Blamey who taught soldiers how to turn an empty bottle into a drinking glass by means of a kerosene-soaked string tied around the middle of the bottle and set alight; the bottle was then plunged into water and broke neatly and cleanly.

LATRINOGRAM a rumour; sometimes *latrine wireless*.

MANDRAKE waterproof cape worn by soldiers in the tropics, from the black cape worn by Mandrake the Magician in the comic strip of the same name.

NACKEROO a member of the North Australian Observer Unit (a play on the more familiar 'jackaroo', substituting the N from 'north').

NIP a Japanese soldier; picked up from the Americans, it began as an abbreviation of *Nippon* (the Japanese word for Japan).

NIPPO Aussie variation on *Nip*, with the distinctive Aussie 'O' ending added.

REHAB rehabilitation of wounded soldiers, sailor and airmen, and of returned servicemen (and women).

REO reinforcements; may have been coined in the First World War, but became a common and popular term in the Second.

SANGO a sandwich; after the war this tended to morph into *sanger*.

SLAP-HAPPY another of the 'happy' crowd (see *bomb-happy*, *flak-happy* and *jungle-happy*); used by Americans before the war for a boxer whose brains were addled by too many fights; used by Aussies during World War II for the mental exhaustion caused by being in too many battles in rapid succession.

SPINEBASHING either sleeping or loafing.

SPINEBASHER the useless oaf who does a lot of this.

STOOGING of aircraft that is cruising around on patrol, not in actual combat; sometimes in the form of *stooging around*.

TOJO a Japanese soldier, alternative to *Nip* or *Nippo* from Hideki Tojo, both Prime Minister of Japan for the duration of World War II and a general in the Imperial Japanese Army.

TOJO-LAND Japan (from the same source as the above).

TROPPO driven barmy by the heat, the humidity, the insects, and the endless jungle (the same symptoms as displayed by those who are *jungle-happy*).

TROPPO (TO GO) to be driven right off your nut by all of the above.

URGER someone who exploits others; it began on Australian racetracks referring to those touts who were always 'urging' hapless punters to back this or that nag; broadened out in the Second World War to cover any and every con man in general.

WAAFERY the part of any air base occupied by the women of the WAAAF ('Women's Auxiliary Australian Air Force').

WOULDN'T IT! an anguished cry of disgust, dismay or frustration.

YANK-HAPPY said of an Australian woman favouring the company of American servicemen ('She's gone mad over the Yanks, that one').

14

THE AUSTRALIAN LANGUAGE

While Aussie English was jauntily bouncing along – playing with words and language as if it didn't have a care in the world – there were those who were keeping an eye on what was going on, and taking notes as they did so (perhaps with the intention of producing them in evidence should the behaviour of this odd lingo ever be called into question).

In fact, the Australian language was being closely observed and reported on almost from the moment it was born. Even as convicts were still shuffling around in leg-irons (the original whingeing Poms) James Hardy Vaux was compiling his vocabulary of 'the flash language'.

Then throughout the nineteenth century our vigorous new

dialect was being noticed and commented on. There is evidence that our distinctive accent had already developed by the 1830s (more on this in chapter 17). In 1882 the *Sydney Slang Dictionary* appeared. There is no author's name on the book, but the very fact of its appearance is what is significant.

By the time the nineteenth century was drawing to a close James Murray was beavering away at what was to become the *Oxford English Dictionary* and our particular dialect of English had grown to maturity and spread across the continent. As already recorded in these pages, Professor EE Morris applied his academic brain to our language, shipping samples to Murray in Oxford and publishing his own pioneering *Dictionary of Austral English*.

As the years went on, writers from CJ Dennis to WH Dowling and beyond faithfully recorded the less formal and more unofficial bits of our language – the bits that the stuffy Professor Morris had left out of his dictionary. Then, as the Second World War drew to a close, Sid Baker focused a new and more powerful spotlight on Australian English.

Sidney J Baker (his preferred by-line) was obsessed (there's no other word for it) with collecting and explaining the Australian language – and he wasn't even born here! He was born Sidney John Baker in Wellington, New Zealand, in 1912. He crossed the Tasman in 1935 and spent most of the rest of his life earning a crust as a journalist on a string of Australian papers: Sydney's *Daily Telegraph*, the Bathurst *National Advocate*, the *ABC Weekly*, the Melbourne *Herald*, the *Sun News-Pictorial* and the *Sydney Morning Herald* among them.

I didn't realise until I spoke to his daughter Suzanne that for most of his adult life (he died in 1976) Sid suffered from multiple sclerosis. That made him a very courageous, if occasionally crotchety and irascible, man. And he comes into our story because of his unending fascination with Aussie English.

The first edition of his great book *The Australian Language* appeared in 1945 as the Second World War was drawing a close and as all those words coined during that conflict were coming home to roost. In 1966 a second, and much revised and rewritten edition, appeared.

Now you have to bear in mind that lexicography (the art and science of writing dictionaries) did not have a high profile in Australia in the days when Sid Baker began putting pen to paper. The situation today is far different (a story we'll tell in chapter 19). But at the time when Baker began writing there was a distinct lack of respect for Australian words and what Australians were doing with them.

By way of example, in 1935 the University of Adelaide appointed an Oxford man as their Jury Professor of English. JIM Stewart (or John Innes Mackintosh Stewart, to give him his full, and very Scottish, name) had studied English literature at Oriel College, Oxford. And it was English literature that he lectured on in Adelaide. Until, that is, he was asked to deliver the 1940 Commonwealth Literary Fund lectures.

He famously began his first lecture with these words: 'I am most grateful to the CLF for providing the funds to give these lectures in Australian literature, but unfortunately they have neglected to provide any literature – I will lecture therefore on DH Lawrence's *Kangaroo*.'

Pow! A sharp right jab in the eye for anyone who thought Australia literature, and Australian English, worth a second glance. Henry Lawson, Banjo Paterson, Rolf Boldrewood,

Marcus Clarke, Katharine Susannah Prichard, Miles Franklin, Joseph Furphy, Henry Handel Richardson and the rest all wiped off the map with one swift backhander. That gives you an idea of the climate into which Sid Baker boldly strode declaring that the Australian language was rich and colourful and well worth recording.

In the second edition of *The Australian Language*, published in 1966, Sid explains how his vision had widened and deepened since the first edition of 1945. Back then, he tells us, he 'thought of it mainly in terms of slang – of words and phrases in popular use which were outside "standard" or "approved" English'. But over time he'd come to see that Australian English is much more that its slang: it's also (he tells us) found in such standard, even commonplace, words such as *lay-by* and *home unit*, in the uniquely Australian distinction between a *Prime Minister* and a *Premier* and in such local coinages as *shark meshing*, *Granny Smith apple* and *woolshed*.

The second edition of Sid's book runs to an impressive 500 pages, but it's not a dictionary dealing with our words alphabetically. Instead, he hacks through the dense (and at the time largely unexplored) undergrowth of Australian English in a series of themed chapters dealing with: The Soil, The Bush, The Road, The City, The Underworld, The Vulgarism, The Young and so on.

In the course of doing so he picks up and examines the gems of Aussie English, rejoicing in their bright and colourful sparkle and trying to work out just where they came from.

For example, Sid turns his attention to *Buckley's chance*. This is first recorded in *The Bulletin* in 1895. It's often shortened to just *Buckley's*, as in 'You've got Buckley's mate!' The

Australian National Dictionary notes that there is a possibility (a very slim possibility, in fact) that the expression comes from a convict named William Buckley, who escaped in 1803 and lived among Victorian Aboriginal communities for thirty-two years. He was known as the 'wild white man'. The problem, as Sid points out, is this Buckley lived from 1780 to 1856 and the expression doesn't appear in print until thirty-nine years after his death – a substantial gap. Plus there is another Buckley who is much more likely to be the source. In my *Dictionary of Australian Phrase and Fable* I tell the story:

> **Buckley's chance** no chance at all. In 1851, a certain Mr Mars Buckley, in partnership with one Crumpton Nunn, set up a store in a small shack in Melbourne. The business of Buckley and Nunn flourished. Then in 1893 a depression hit Melbourne and there was a run on the banks. Wily old Mars Buckley, accompanied by four assistants carrying leather suitcases, pushed through the crowds around the bank (who were demanding their money) and withdrew 10 000 gold sovereigns which he then locked away in a safe in his shop – leaving no chance that the bank might fritter away his fortune among other anxious depositors. Two years later, in 1895, the expression 'Buckley's chance' first appeared in print, leading to the expression that you have two chances: 'Buckley's or none' – both a play on the name of the shop, and a reference to Mars Buckley being the only winner on the day he withdrew all the cash from the bank.

The problem with my story is that it would make *Buckley's chance* a good chance (not a bad one) since it was Mr Buckley who ended up with the gold. Mind you, it might have started out with a positive meaning and reversed as time went on. However, there are no citations to support such a reversal, so we turn to Sid for his judgment.

Sid Baker takes the view that the expression comes simply from the name of the old Melbourne firm of Buckley & Nunn, and that it began life in the longer form of 'You've got two chances mate – *Buckley's or none*' as an intentional play on words. In this, as in so many other examples, Sid is almost certainly right.

This shows us that Sidney J Baker was not a man to duck away from the difficult and puzzling questions, and not reluctant to form an opinion and defend it (unlike so many academics who end their quest with 'maybe this' or then again 'maybe that').

Mind you, when a disputed or doubtful term crossed his path Sid Baker was properly sceptical. The word *wowser* is a case in point. I think of a *wowser* as someone who draws a line in the sand of moral judgment, but in Australia it became a term of general abuse – either because some people thought the line was in the wrong place or because they thought there should be no line at all demarking moral from immoral.

The word *wowser* was especially associated with the old Sydney *Truth* newspaper, whose colourful editor John Norton (1858–1916) railed angrily (often in alliterative headlines) against any criticism of an indulgent lifestyle (a lifestyle he famously practised as well as preached). Sid quotes one of Norton's typical headlines (from 1899): 'Willoughby Wowsers Worried'.

But when Norton claimed to have coined the word *wowser* from a phrase of his own invention ('We Only Want Social Evils

Remedied') Sid rightly smelled a rat. He knew that most of the claims that an established word is the product of an acronym are false (not all, but most). In fact, *wowser* almost certainly derives from an older English dialect expression, 'to wow', meaning to howl or whine like a dog. Baker was never a sucker for what are called 'folk etymologies' – fanciful (invented) stories about word origins.

Jumbuck is another of those puzzling expressions. Every Australian knows the word from Banjo Paterson's 'Waltzing Matilda':

> Down came a jumbuck to drink at the waterhole,
> Up jumped the swagman and grabbed him with glee;
> And he sang as he put him away in his tucker-bag,
> 'You'll come a-waltzing matilda with me.'

The context makes it clear that what's being spoken about here is a sheep the swagman intends to barbecue – it's a nice bit of roast mutton he has in mind. But how did a sheep come to be called a *jumbuck*? I've already suggested it might an Aboriginal pidgin word – a corruption of 'jump up'.

The *Australian National Dictionary* takes the cautious approach and says 'of unknown origin' but then tentatively suggests it might be a pidgin word – an alteration or corruption (as I said) of 'jump up'. But in its entry on *jump up* the *AND* says the expression means 'to come back to life; especially in the phrase "to jump up whitefellow", [meaning] to be reincarnated as a white person'. But how in earth do you get from *that* meaning to the leaping behaviour of sheep?

Which brings us back to Sid Baker – who is convinced that

jumbuck is not a pidgin word at all, but a real word from an Aboriginal language. In support of this contention he quotes the Australian poet Charles Harpur (1813–68). Sid had tracked down a handwritten note in Harpur's papers in the Mitchell Library in Sydney. In the note Harpur talks about the Aboriginal word *junbuc* or possibly *jinbuc* (his writing, Sid notes, is not very clear). Here's the quotation in full:

> an Aboriginal name for a shag-haired species of Kangaroo peculiar to mountain copses. It may be called the mountain wallaby, being in relation to the wallaroo what the common wallaby is to the Kangaroo proper. The 'junbuc' [or 'jinbuc'] is the least elegant in its form, and the dullest in its nature, of all the Kangaroo kinds – of all such at least as I happen to be acquainted with. The Blacks of the Hunter call sheep 'junbuc' [or 'jinbuc'] no doubt from a resemblance, however remote, arising out the hairy shagginess of the one and the woolliness of the other.

From this Sid Baker became firmly convinced that *jumbuck* is a word of Aboriginal origin and not a pidgin-like twisting of an English expression. And he's not reluctant to take on the academic scholars. He fired a shot across the bows of Bill Ramson's essay, 'The Currency of Aboriginal Words in English' (1964), for daring to suggest that *jumbuck* is 'pidgin when it is, in fact, an Aboriginal word'.

I should add that it is true that there are small, shaggy-haired wallabies (those that live in the centre of Australia are known in the local language as *mala*). So Charles Harpur's note may be entirely correct. However, there is still room for debate.

In fact, as Sid Baker so often demonstrated, there is always room for debate when you're discussion something as lively and colourful as Aussie English. This is what makes his great book of such compelling interest: it's a combination of his diligent (obsessive) research, with his determined (even stubborn) character.

I should add that despite the shot Sid fired at the great Australian lexicographer Bill Ramson in the comment noted above, it was Ramson who wrote the generous entry on Sid for the *Australian Dictionary of Biography*. In that entry Ramson describes Sid as 'a frail figure, bespectacled and bearded … increasingly handicapped, though never defeated, and never idle'. And of Sid's singleminded focus on understanding our language, Ramson says: 'it was Baker's "magnificent obsession" … that ensures his honoured place as an Australianist'.

Later Bill Ramson was to edit the magisterial *Australian National Dictionary* (that story is told in chapter 19) in which he gives us this definition of *Australianist*: 'Pride in or loyalty to Australian nationalism; a character distinctively Australian'. That was Sid Baker: born a Kiwi, became one of us, and gave us a monumental record of how we write and speak in *The Australian Language*.

While Sid Baker was diligently at work, keeping his notes and doing his research, another man was also paying close attention to Aussie English as she is spoke – a man with a remarkably acute ear for what was actually happening in Australian conversational English. His name was John O'Grady and it's to his story that we now turn.

WORD LIST

Sid Baker's masterpiece is out of print these days, but if you should ever find a copy in a second-hand bookshop seize upon it at once! (I'm not suggesting you smuggle it out of the shop – pay for it first.) You will find much pleasure in its pages. And here are some of the words to which Sid devoted his attention.

ANCHOR, TO HIT THE to slam on the car brakes.

APPLES all right or satisfactory as in 'How's it going?' 'She's apples' (from the rhyming slang of 'apples and spice' = 'nice').

ASPHALT our word for what Americans call *bitumen* (always pronounced 'ash-felt').

BIG DITCH, THE the Darling River.

BIG-NOTE YOURSELF, TO to boast (our mothers always told us 'don't big-note yourself').

BLOCK, TO DO YOUR to become angry.

BOILOVER an unexpected win by a long-priced outsider in a horse race.

BOWER BIRD a person who is an obsessive hoarder (usually of rubbish or small trinkets).

BUNGERS fireworks that exploded (rather than producing a shower of sparks).

BURN OFF, TO (1) to race in a car or motorbike or, among children, on a pushbike; (2) to back-burn in the bush as a form of bushfire prevention.

BUSHED (1) confused; (2) exhausted; (3) lost.

COATHANGER the Sydney Harbour Bridge (at first applied mockingly by Melburnians, later adopted with pride by Sydneysiders).

COCKIE farmer (on a smaller scale than a pastoralist or squatter).

COLOUR the flash of opal found in opal-bearing rock (or silica).

CRACKER NIGHT the one night of the year when backyard fireworks were allowed (the last Cracker Night in New South Wales was 7 June 1986, after which fireworks were banned for safety reasons).

CRACKERS fireworks.

CROCKERY false teeth.

DEAD DUCK (1) someone who fails badly; (2) a task or project that has failed.

DIRTY BIG a mild expletive (as in 'you're a dirty big liar') – used mainly by children.

DRUNK AS CHLOE, AS very drunk, possibly from the famous full-length painting of a naked young woman (known as 'Chloe') in the bar of Young & Jackson's Hotel in Melbourne.

DUMPER a wave that breaks with unexpected violence on the shore.

GOER, A (1) a horse whose jockey is honestly trying to win a race; (2) a woman who is free and easy with her sexual favours.

PRAWNHEAD a foolish person, or one with the IQ of a gum tree.

SESSION, A a period of time spent drinking.

SHAVING MONEY a very small amount of money (underworld slang).

SLUG, TO to overcharge.

SOUTHERLY BUSTER a strong breeze from the south.

STINK, A an uproar, a noisy complaint (as in 'kicking up a stink').

STUNNED MULLET someone who is said to *look like a stunned mullet* is either (1) slack-jawed and speechless with astonishment; or (2) unconscious.

YAK AND NO YAKKA, ALL all talk and no action.

15

THE WORDS
OF THE
WEIRD MOB

Publishers tend to be a lean and haggard-looking lot (it comes from mixing with authors). But in the 1950s one Australian publisher had reason to puff contentedly on his pipe and open up the best port. His name was Sydney Ure Smith. He was the second of that name and was, at the time, running the publishing house founded by his father.

In 1957 he had a publishing phenomenon on his hands – a title that exploded across Australia. The book was a comic novel called *They're a Weird Mob* by Nino Culotta. Ure Smith produced an initial print run of 6000 hardback copies. For the time that was a generous first printing – so Sydney (or 'Sam' as he was known to his friends) must have had confidence in this unusual book. Just how right he was quickly became apparent.

In less than six months, the book had been reprinted eight times and sold 74 000 copies. By the end of its first year in print over 130 000 copies had been sold. (Bear in mind that at the time the population of Australia was less than ten million – making those sales figures astonishing.) Also in those early years *They're a Weird Mob* was serialised in newspapers and on radio and was read aloud by an actor on late night television. By the time its author died twenty-four years later it had sold well over 900 000 copies. Not bad for a comic novel from an unknown writer.

So who was this author with the Italian-sounding name, and why was the book so popular? Well, the author was in reality a restless, loud, boisterous Irish-Australian named John O'Grady (1907–81), and attributing authorship to 'Nino Culotta' was part of the joke.

The comic yarn, narrated in the first person by this imaginary Italian, told of a visitor to Australia from the north of Italy (from Piedmont) at a time when, in those years following the Second World War, migrants from the Mediterranean end of Europe were flooding into Australia in large numbers.

The book tells the story of Giovanni, known as 'Nino', Culotta, a magazine journalist sent by his employer to write a series of articles about Australians and the Australian way of life to give Italian readers an idea of how their relatives were faring in Australia and what life was like here.

In order to discover the real, everyday Australians, Nino takes a job as a builder's labourer working for a small-time Bankstown builder named Joe Kennedy. Nino gets to know his employer and his workmates and discovers that the formal English he learned in school doesn't work in conversations with ordinary Aussies.

The plot of the book is a simple romantic comedy. Nino meets Kay in a cafe in Manly trying to eat spaghetti with a spoon. His, at first unwelcome, lesson in how to eat spaghetti properly sparks a lively relationship that ends in marriage – with Nino abandoning his job as a journalist and settling in Australia permanently.

The humour of the book comes from the language. Early in the book Nino makes the following observation:

> Most Australians speak English like I speak Hindustani, which
> I don't. In general, they use English words, but in a way
> that makes no sense to anyone else. And they don't use our
> European vowel sounds, so that even if they do construct a
> normal sentence, it doesn't sound like one.

The story is told mainly in dialogue with John O'Grady (as Nino) setting out to capture in print the flavour of the distinctive Aussie dialect. The enormous popularity of the book came from his success in this project. For many readers it was the first time they had encountered the contemporary conversational language of ordinary Aussies captured and reproduced so faithfully. What O'Grady had was an uncannily accurate ear. He heard what was actually happening in Australian English, remembered it, and wrote it down.

They're a Weird Mob delighted its first readers with the shock of recognition. It was, for those early readers, as if they had just encountered a mirror and seen their own reflection for the first time. O'Grady's acute ear, his sharp intelligence, and his widely wandering lifestyle had (perhaps uniquely) equipped him to show us how we really spoke.

John Patrick O'Grady was born in 1907 in the Sydney suburb of Waverley. His father gave up a job in the New South Wales Department of Lands to go farming, taking up an isolated mixed farm on the Peel River, near Tamworth in northern New South Wales. Young John was educated at home, then as a boarder at St Stanislaus' College, Bathurst. From there he went to Sydney University, graduating as a pharmacist.

He tried his hand at running his own small pharmacy, first in Mudgee, then in Ballina. Both went broke (it was the time of the Great Depression). So he sold out and worked as a travelling salesman for a pharmaceutical company – a job that took as him the length and breadth of Australia (regularly crossing the Nullarbor to Perth).

In the Second World War John O'Grady served in the Australian Army Medical Corps, rising to the rank of temporary captain and serving as pharmacist on the hospital ship *Manunda*. After the war he took a variety of jobs. (At one stage he owned the fish and chip shop next to the Oatley pub.) Bored by the routine work of an ordinary suburban pharmacy, he took a New Zealand government job as a pharmacist in Western Samoa. It was while he was in New Zealand waiting for this appointment to be finalised that he finished writing *They're a Weird Mob*.

He'd been slogging away at the book for some years. Every few days he'd visit his son (also named John, also to become a successful writer) and pace up and down his son's small living room reading aloud the most recent chapters. With the final chapters finished during his time in New Zealand, he posted the completed manuscript to young John with instructions to 'sling it in a drawer 'til I get back'. His son cheerfully disobeyed these instructions and sent the book to Angus & Robertson (who rejected it) and then to Sydney Ure Smith (who could spot a gold mine when he saw one).

And all of John O'Grady's colourful, and widespread, life experiences played into the remarkable success of the book: the breadth of his travels across the country, the wide range of Australians of all classes and ranks that he met, and the actual writing taking place across the Tasman where he was very aware of those distinctive Australian voices he was missing.

He wrote the Aussie dialect he delighted in with the same pleasure that Robbie Burns felt for his Scottish dialect, or CJ Dennis the dialect of the inner-city, larrikin, working-class Australians at the start of the twentieth century.

After Nino's first day of working on a building site for Joe Kennedy, Joe takes him home for dinner to meet his wife Edie. Also present is another of Joe's workers, Jimmy, who boards with Joe and Edie:

> Joe indicated one of the chairs, 'Sit down, Nino. Take a load orf yer feet.' Then he raised his voice. 'Yer there, Edie?' A woman's voice answered from somewhere out the back. He said, 'Come 'ere. We got a visitor for tea.'
>
> The voice shouted, 'Who is it?'
>
> 'You don' know 'im. Come 'ere an' meet 'im.'
>
> She appeared. A slim woman of about Joe's age and colouring. I rose to my feet.
>
> Joe said, 'Nino, this is my wife Edie. Edie, this is Nino. He's

just started with us. He's Italian. He's orright, though.'

Edie said, 'Pleased to meet you.'

I said, 'How do you do, Mrs. Joe.'

'Don' call 'er Mrs. Joe. Call 'er Edie. Wot's for tea, Ede?'

'I got some fish. And there's some beans and potatoes.'

'Fair enough. How long will ut be?'

'It's cooked now.'

'Good on yer, Ede. Enough ter go round?'

'I always have enough on Fridays. I never know how many there'll be.'

'Just the four us. 'Ave a drink with us before tea?'

'Wouldn't mind.'

She sat on the sofa and folded her hands. Jimmy sat beside her and began rolling a cigarette.

Then Edie said, 'Is Betty coming over, Jimmy?'

'Yeah.'

'How is she?'

'Orright.'

You get the flavour. And the first readers simply fell in love with a book that sounded just like ordinary Aussies talking.

John O'Grady had, as I said, an acute ear for the sound of spoken Aussie English. And one of the things he noticed was how ordinary Aussies used the word *bloody*. At the time it was often referred to as the 'great Australian adjective' – even though it wasn't, strictly speaking, an Australian word at all. The *Oxford English Dictionary* tells us *bloody* is recorded from 1676 (long before the English language had even set sail for our shores) as 'a vague epithet expressing anger, resentment, detestation; but often as a mere intensive'.

The term probably comes from an earlier use of the word *blood* to refer to the sons of the nobility (because they were of good blood, well descended). And these young bloods were, apparently a wild, heavy-drinking crowd. Hence the expression *drunk as a blood* was born (cf. *drunk as a lord*) – and in time this became *bloody drunk*. This is probably the source of the adjectival use that began in England and was adopted in Australia.

So why did it come to be thought of as an especially Australian expression?

For two reasons. First because of the frequency of its use – scattered richly through many spoken sentences as a flavouring agent, rather like grated parmesan heaped on spaghetti. And secondly because of the way it was integrated into other words and phrases – an integration possibly unique to Australia.

This integration is recorded at the beginning of *They're a Weird Mob* when Nino is driven from the docks (he has just arrived on a migrant ship) by a taxi driver:

> After a while, he said, 'Well we can't sit 'ere all bloody day; where we goin'?'
>
> I was silently translating what he said into what I thought he meant in an English I understood, and translating this into Italian, to be translated into English, all of which was taking some time, when he suddenly seemed to become very irritable and said, 'Gawd I've been drivin' this bloody thing since one o'bloody-clock this mornin' an' now it's bloody near time for lunch an' I 'ave to get landed with a bloody ning nong who doesn't know where 'e's bloody goin'. Will the Cross do yer?'

By the time I had worked out a few words of this speech, we had arrived somewhere, and he was getting my bags out of the boot. I got out also, and said, 'Excuse me, sir, but do you mind telling me where I now am?'

'Kings Cross. Three bob.'

'Excuse me, sir, but do you mind telling me where I now am?'

He shouted very loudly, 'Kings Bloody Cross!'

From this exchange Nino assumes that the correct name for the location is 'Kings Bloody Cross' – which is how he keeps on referring to it until corrected by a policeman in a later chapter:

He thought for a moment. 'Who told you that was its name?'

'The taxi driver.'

'What taxi driver?'

I told him about my arrival and the taxi driver. He laughed very much. He said, 'Leave the bloody out. That's a swear word in this country. Its name is just Kings Cross.'

Of course, many Australian conversations ignore the policeman's friendly advice. And John O'Grady famously wrote a poem about the great Australian adjective entitled 'The Integrated Adjective'. A few lines will give you the flavour:

An' the other bloke said, 'Seen 'im. Owed 'im 'alf a bloody quid.

Forgot to give it back to 'im; but now I bloody did.

Coulda used the thing me-bloody-self; been orf the bloody booze,

Up at Tumba-bloody-rumba shootin' kanga-bloody-roos.'

Brilliant though this observation (and its expression) is, O'Grady was not the first to notice it. As we've already seen, CJ Dennis had done something similar in his poem 'The Austral-aise'. In fact, it seems to me that the mantle of Dennis, the great pioneer of Australian dialect writing, fell upon the shoulders of John O'Grady, and that he was a worthy inheritor of that tradition.

In 1966 *They're a Weird Mob* was turned into a movie by the famous English film-making team of Michael Powell and Emeric Pressburger (the people who made such notable films as *Colonel Blimp*, *49th Parallel*, *One of Our Aircraft is Missing* and *Black Narcissus*). The movie was shot on location at Punchbowl, Circular Quay, Bondi and Manly beaches, Martin Place and across Sydney. It starred Italian actor Walter Chiari as Nino, Ed Devereaux as his boss Joe, Slim DeGrey and John Meillon as his workmates Pat and Dennis, Clare Dunn as his love inter-est Kay, and legendary Australian actor Chips Rafferty as her father. Unsurprisingly the movie was a huge box office success in Australia, although according to some reports O'Grady was not entirely happy with it.

O'Grady went on to write another eighteen books, but none enjoyed the success of *They're a Weird Mob* – which had succeeded in giving Australians a fresh and startled sense of self-recognition in his ingenious recording of our own distinctive dialect.

I interviewed John O'Grady on my radio show when he was promoting one of his later books, *Aussie English: An Explanation of Australian Idiom*. I found him to be the energetic, boisterous Irish-Australian suggested by his reputation, and just as inter-ested as ever in the words Australians were using and we how were using them.

In our conversation he insisted that not only do we have our own special dialect of English, but it's an English most other English speakers find difficult to understand. Given the more recent success of some Australian movies and TV soapies overseas this is, perhaps, no longer true. He also expressed the view that (compared to other English-speaking countries) Australia has almost no regional dialects – with minor variations, he said, we speak the same pretty much everywhere.

On the subject of our accent he was not very flattering. 'There's no music in the Australian accent,' he told me, comparing the way we sound to the tuneless bleating of sheep or the pathetic cry of a lonely crow (more on our accent in chapter 17).

O'Grady also pointed out (and all his books demonstrate) that Aussies are extremely inventive where language is concerned – and part of the fun of talking to Aussies, he said, is listening for new expressions, new combinations, and new ways of saying things.

Which brings us to one special quality of Australian English – namely our inclination to take perfectly good words and shrink them into something smaller and neater. It's to that Aussie linguistic habit that we now turn.

WORD LIST

John O'Grady was a great observer and recorder of the lingo of the ordinary Aussie. So what kinds of words did he pick up on? Here's a small sample:

<u>ACID</u> *to put the acid on* is to ask a woman for her sexual favours.

<u>ACT, BUNGING ON AN</u> pretending to be what one is not.

<u>BACK, GET OFF MY</u> stop annoying me.

<u>BATTLER</u> (1) someone struggling in life; (2) an ordinary Aussie.

<u>BEAUT!</u> Excellent!

<u>BEER</u> warm and weak in England, cold and strong in Australia.

<u>BITE</u> *to put the bite on* is to ask for a favour (or for money).

<u>BLACK STUMP</u> a mythical place so far away that anything that's *beyond the black stump* is unimaginably distant.

<u>BLOCK, TO DO YOUR</u> to lose your temper.

<u>BLOW-IN</u> an unwanted stranger.

<u>BOMB</u> a very old car.

<u>BOOZER</u> a pub.

<u>BOTTLER</u> some person or thing that's very good is a bottler (from *your blood's worth bottling mate*).

<u>CROOK</u> sick; sometimes you might be *butchers* which is rhyming slang ('butcher's hook' = crook); if you're very sick you're as *crook as Rookwood* (well-known Sydney cemetery).

<u>DEKKO</u> to look; 'have a dekko at this mate'.

<u>DEMON</u> a plain clothes police officer, a detective.

DIRTY, TO COME THE to use unfair tactics.

DOB IN to inform on someone (Aussies strongly disapprove of dobbing anyone in).

DODGER bread.

DUD no good; doesn't work.

DUMP an unpleasant, untidy place ('you wouldn't be seen dead in that dump!').

EDGE, HAVING THE if you have the edge on someone you have an advantage over them.

FAIR GO reasonableness, sportsmanship, justice (the basis of much Australian moral thinking).

FANG *putting the fangs on* someone is trying to borrow money from them.

FIZZLE failing, fading out, eventually ceasing to exist.

FULL (1) eaten too much; (2) had too much alcohol to drink.

GONE A MILLION caught out; trapped; your deception has been seen through.

GUTSER, COME A having your plans fail.

ICKY sticky (possibly embarrassing) situation.

KICK IN help pay for.

KNOCK, TO to criticise.

LASH, TO HAVE A to make an attempt; to try.

LOAF, TO to do nothing.

MUG a bloke who hasn't got a clue.

NIGGLY irritable; bad-tempered.

OPEN SLATHER no restrictions; an open go.

POOPED exhausted.

PUNT, TO HAVE A originally to have a bet, but now it means to have a go at anything; to make an attempt.

RATBAG an eccentric person; a lot of the most interesting Australians are genuine ratbags.

RUBBISH, TO to insult; to denigrate; to put down.

SHIRTY irritable; in a bad mood.

SHOOT THROUGH, TO to leave abruptly.

TOGS clothes, e.g. work togs, swimming togs, etc.

WHINGE, TO to complain.

WOG an infection; anything from serious influenza to a slight head cold.

16

THE
INCREDIBLE
SHRINKING
WORDS

The *tall poppy syndrome* refers to the Australian habit of cutting self-important people down to size. So adept are we at this particular exercise that we even do it to language. Many an inflated word has been strutting around our nation, smug and self-assured because of how many syllables it contained, when a quick snip with the Aussie verbal scissors reduced it to a bonsai version of its former self. This is the story of how that happens. It's the story of how Aussie English shrinks words.

In 1956 American science fiction writer Richard Matheson published a novel called *The Shrinking Man*. The following year Hollywood turned it into one of those classic black-and-white science fiction horror movies of the 1950s by adding an adjective to the title. It became *The Incredible Shrinking Man*.

Both the book and the movie tell the story of an American businessman, named Scott Carey, who is on board his yacht off the coast of California when he is enveloped in a strange (presumably radioactive) mist. In the weeks that follow he discovers that he is slowly shrinking in size. This remarkable phenomenon cannot be arrested. He ends up living in the dolls' house in his own home and being attacked by his own cat. Later, trapped in the basement of his house he does battle with a (to him) gigantic, voracious spider and the movie ends with him looking forward (if that's the right way to put it) to shrinking down to sub-atomic size.

The point is that Aussie English performs much the same function on words that the mysterious mist performed on Scott Carey. Generations of Australians have been shrinking words, and the process seems to continue with each new generation that comes along.

The man who has devoted many years to studying this phenomenon and recording the results is Emeritus Professor Roly Sussex of the University of Queensland (where he held the chair of Applied Language Studies). Although he was born and educated in England, Roly has long been a fixture on the Australian language landscape. For many years he hosted the *Language Talkback* program on ABC Radio and ran an associated 'Language Talkback' website. Retired from his university chair he still presents *A Word in Your Ear* on ABC Radio and writes the 'Wordlimit' column for the *Courier-Mail* newspaper.

Like a bower bird or magpie collecting brightly coloured things, Roly has been collecting Aussie colloquialisms, especially diminutives, for many years – from curiosity and from his love for the language. He tells me that his list of diminutives now runs to well over 5000 entries. Clearly we are serious about shrinking the language!

There are, Roly tells me, several reasons why we do this word shrinking. In part it is a move towards making our language more informal. But it's also a matter of 'solidarity' – the way Aussies talk to each about the things we know, like and share. This makes diminutives 'identifiers' – small verbal signals that we all belong to the same mob.

So if I invite you to a *barbecue* at my place that's being rather formal, but if I invite you to a *barbie* it's both friendlier and shows solidarity (it shows that we both belong to the same language 'club'). Roly says that Australians in Earls Court, in London, will use this sort of language even more than they would at home – precisely because they are out of their home territory and they want to emphasise the fact that they belong together.

Another factor, says Roly, in the creation of Aussie diminutives is the pleasure we seem to take in playing with language.

'We are supposed to be a bit laconic,' he says, 'but we are also famous for being inventive and colourful in language – "flat out like a lizard drinking", all that kind of thing. And I think these diminutives are part of the way we like playing with words because we are inveterate tinkerers with the language around us. That's where you get expressions like "as useless as a flyscreen in a submarine" or "portholes in a coffin" and so on. There are hundreds of these inventions in Australian English.'

There is a history, says Roly, of Australians being aware of, and taking an interest in, the language around us: 'Australian English has always been on the lookout for interesting ways to say things. We've sucked up words from everywhere – including a lot of Aboriginal words.'

So if you put those factors together – informality, solidarity and inventiveness – you get an idea of why Aussies take such pleasure in shrinking words.

So, how do we go about it? How do we shrink our words? Often we cut two or three syllables back to one and then add an 'a' sound, an 'ee' sound or an 'oh' sound. Roly tells me that Aussies have about twenty-four different ways of constructing diminutives, but to my ear these three are the most common.

In fact, the most famous diminutive of all is formed this way. *Aussie* was born in the First World War. The earliest citation for the shortened word in the *Australian National Dictionary* is from 1915, and refers to the country, not the person. There was even a magazine called *Aussie* – printed 'in the field' says the front cover, 'by the AIF' as the Australian Soldiers' Magazine, from 1918. Then from 1920 a civilian (commercial) version appeared as *Aussie: 'The Cheerful Monthly'* (it survived until 1932). By then the word *Aussie* had been firmly cemented into our national life – and we've been Aussies ever since.

Then if you think about the possibility that you might work as a *brickie*, get up early for *brekkie* and owe money to the *bookie* it's clear that we have a heap of these words ending in the 'ee' sound (without even leaving the first two letters of the alphabet!)

In fact, the majority of diminutives on Roly's massive database end with the 'ee' sound (spelled with a 'y' or an 'ie').

'The convenience of this,' he says, 'can be seen in a word such as *firie*, meaning a fire officer, because it's gender neutral – the fire fighter concerned may be either male or female. *Postie* is another example. *Ambo* works in the same way, because so many ambulance officers are now female.'

Which brings us to all the diminutives that end in 'o' – and there are many of them (like the *ambo* just mentioned). Perhaps the most famous is *arvo* meaning 'afternoon', which can sometimes become *'Sarvo* meaning 'This afternoon' (well, why bother with more syllables than you need?) In the list at the end of this chapter are many examples – from going *berko* to having a *smoko*.

Then there are placenames. Some of these we just chop down, so that Coff's Harbour becomes *Coff's*, the Sydney suburb of Paddington becomes *Paddo* and in north Queensland Rockhampton becomes *Rocky*. The other thing Aussie word-shrinking can sometimes do to placenames is to make them a bit more musical. Thus the Hong Kong and Shanghai Bank came to be called the *Honkers and Shonkers*. In other examples the definite article is added to the front of the name – as in the case of *The Isa* and *The Alice*.

Shrinking a placename is a way, says Roly, of indicating an amiable familiarity with the place – even an affection for it.

When it comes to shrinking personal names it seems we have a fancy for adding a 'za' ending, as in: *Bazza* (Barry), *Gazza* (Garry) and *Kazza* (Karen) – along with a host of similar constructions. But even that shrinking hasn't gone far enough, so we then shrink those diminutives down to *Baz* and *Gaz* and *Kaz*.

Roly says: 'Every language that I've looked at – and I've checked out about sixty – has got diminutives for people's first names. Slavonic languages have many ways of changing or shortening people's names. So Chekov's Uncle Vanya is actually a form of Ivan. But they don't do it nearly as much for other things as we do. We do it not just with people and places but even with vegetables, so that a cucumber becomes a *cue* or a *cuie* or a *cuke* and an avocado becomes an *avo*. We even do it for adjectives such as *bewdy*. No other language seems to shrink words quite as much as Australian English does.'

In fact, we even apply our word-shrinking habit to wines (so cabernet sauvignon becomes *cab sav*) and to food (spaghetti bolognese becomes *spag bol*).

And to all of this Roly adds the warning: 'If you don't use these expressions with a friend you sound as if you're having a bad day, or you've been offended by them or something similar.'

Another example is our habit of calling a chicken a *chook*. The only citations for *chook* in the *Oxford English Dictionary* come from Australia and New Zealand and start from the nineteenth century.

Although we spell the word with a double-'o' today, it used to be spelled with a 'u'. The earliest citations in the *Australian National Dictionary* have the 'chuck' spelling. But because it began life as a north of England dialect word, even with that spelling it was probably pronounced as we pronounce chook today. Dr Samuel Johnson, in his *Dictionary of the English Language* (1755), says that *chuck* or *chook* was a familiar term of endearment applied to husbands, wives, children and close companions. This makes sense, since it would be the equivalent of calling a child 'my little chicken'. Dr Johnson also says that *chuck* or *chook* was a dialectal corruption of *chick* (the usual abbreviation of *chicken*). It seems never have caught on in the south of England, and to have largely died out by the late nineteenth century. But by that time the word had been carried to Australia, where we have kept it alive by calling our chickens not *chicks* but *chooks*.

In Australia *chook* is also likely to be the nickname of anyone with the family name of Fowler. It's a joke – a *chook* is a Fowl(er), you see!

As the word shrinking continues, some expressions are reduced to mere initials. Thus being sacked by the boss is being given the *DCM* ('don't come Monday'), and on your feet you're wearing *RMs* – meaning the legendary elastic-sided outback books made by RM Williams. And at least one four-syllable word has been reduced to a single letter of the alphabet – 'kilometres' has become *K's*. (In my observation this is a relatively recent addition to our list of shrunken words, so the process seems to be continuing.)

'Aussie diminutives,' says Roly Sussex, 'used to be restricted to the spoken language but they are now turning up more frequently in the written language as well. For instance, even the London *Times* will use the word *Aussies* to describe the Australian cricket team.'

So are there social and cultural reasons for this compulsive word shrinking? Does it grow out of who we are, and what we are, and how we see ourselves?

'Yes, I think so,' says Sussex. 'For instance, we tend to get onto first-name terms quicker than in any other place I know. I remember living in England for years and the lady upstairs would not acknowledge my morning "Hello" until we'd been introduced by someone who knew us both. After that she would acknowledge me in a gracious way. That kind of thing is almost unimaginable in Australia. And in Australia we expect to use people's first names. In this country if you ask someone what their name is, you expect to hear their first name. If I was a medical doctor in Germany I would expect to be addressed as "Herr Doktor" – which is very formal, and puts a certain distance between us. But in Australia it's not at all unusual for patients to address their GP by the doctor's first name – and quite often in the diminutive, or friendly, form. I would never, for instance, introduce myself as Roland, which sounds a bit medieval and formal, while Roly is appropriately friendly and informal.'

Australians, he says, tend not to take offence if they are addressed by their first name. In fact, if people don't use first names they tend to sound distant and standoffish. 'I think,' he says 'that the flat social structure in Australia – where everyone is as good as everyone else – may have something to do with it.' This 'flat social structure' is captured in JF Archibald's comment that 'I have nothing against Oxford men. Some of our best shearers' cooks are Oxford men'.

Certain tribes in the Amazon rainforest area are known as head-hunters. They display their trophies in the form of shrunken heads. Turning the head of a slain enemy into a shrunken head is a grisly process that involves removing the skull and boiling what remains in water that has been saturated with a number of herbs containing tannins. The head is then dried with hot rocks and sand, while moulding it to retain its human features.

Shrinking words is a much more pleasant, and less lethal, pastime, and one that Aussies will most probably continue to pursue for many years to come. In the trophy case of Aussie English is not a gruesome collection of shrunken heads, with their lips and eyelids sewn together, but a sparkling collection of shrunken words – and the collection continues to grow.

In order to take a look at our habit of shrinking words we have had to step out of the timeline, the narrative, of the history of Australian English. While we're standing here on the banks of the stream, watching the waters of time flow past, we might remain just long enough to take a look at how our distinctive accent has developed, and how it's changed, over the years. So that is what we turn to next.

WORD LIST

Australian diminutives run, as Roly Sussex has discovered, into the thousands. The following is a small sample. There may even be some here you haven't come across before.

ACCA, ACKER, ACCO academic.

ADDERS Adelaide.

ADFA Australian Defence Force Academy (pronounced *add-fer*).

AGGIE (1) agricultural pipe; (2) an agate: a clear marble with a spot of colour in the middle, used in the children's game of marbles; (3) testicles [from the marbles]; (4) agapanthus.

AGGRO (1) aggressive; (2) aggravation.

ALICE, THE Alice Springs.

ALKIE alcoholic.

AMBO (1) ambulance officer; (2) ambulance vehicle.

AMMO ammunition.

ANDERS Andrew.

ANGE Angela.

ARVO afternoon.

ASPRO associate professor.

AUSSIE (1) an Australian person; (2) Australia itself (the nation, the continent).

AVO avocado.

BACH, TO to live as a bachelor.

BANGERS Bangkok.

BAPPO Baptist.

BARBIE barbecue.

BARNSEY Jimmy Barnes (singer).

BARRA barramundi.

BATHERS swimming costume.

BAZZA Barry.

BERKO berserk.

BEWDY beauty ('very good'); a general term of approval.

BILLIES (rhyming slang; the 'billy lids' = the kids).

BILLY billy can (rarely said in full, almost always 'the billy').

BIZZO business (as in 'do the business' = get on with the job).

BOLSHIE short for Bolshevik (meaning someone who is a bit of a stirrer or troublemaker).

BLOWIE blowfly.

BLUEY (1) a swag, from the blue blanket that was the outer wrapping; (2) a blue cattle dog; (3) a fine or summons, from the blue paper on which such documents were once printed; (4) anyone with red hair; (5) a blue-tongue lizard.

BLUNNIES Blundstone boots (legendary Aussie boots, once made in Tasmania).

BOARDIES board-shorts (as worn by surfers).

BOATIE a boating enthusiast.

BOD body.

BOOKIE bookmaker.

BREKKIE breakfast.

BRICKIE bricklayer.

BRIZZIE Brisbane.

BUDGIE budgerigar.

BUNDY (1) Bundaberg rum; (2) the Queensland city of Bundaberg where the rum is made.

CAB SAV cabernet sauvignon.

CARBIE carburettor.

CARDIE cardigan.

CAZZA, CAZZ Caroline.

CHEWIE chewing gum.

CHOOK chicken.

CHRISSIE (1) Christmas; (2) Christine; (3) Christina.

CHRYSANTH chrysanthemum.

CIGGIE, CIG cigarette.

COCKIE (1) cockroach; (2) cockatoo; (3) small farmer (a 'cockatoo farmer').

COFF'S Coff's Harbour.

COLDIE a cold beer.

COMFY comfortable.

COOTA Cootamundra.

COZZIE swimming costume.

CUBBY a child's cubbyhouse.

CUEY, CUKE, CUE cucumber.

CUSHY an easy job (as 'soft as a cushion').

DAFF daffodil.

DCM sacked, fired ('don't come Monday').

DEMO a protest demonstration.

DERO a homeless person (hence a 'derelict').

DIN-DINS dinner (used when speaking to a small child).

DONK engine (usually a car engine, short for 'donkey').

DORRIE Doris.

DOUGIE Douglas.

DOWNER a major disappointment (something makes you feel a bit down, a bit sad).

EKKA (1) the Brisbane Exhibition Ground; (2) the annual agricultural show held there.

FIREY fire fighter.

FROSTIE a cold beer.

HEALS Ian Healy (former Australian wicket keeper).

HENDO anyone named Henderson.

HONKERS Hong Kong.

ISA, THE Mount Isa.

JARMIES pyjamas.

KAZZA, KAZ Karen.

K's kilometres (as in distance travelled).

LACKER elastic band.

LAZZA Larry.

LEGGIE a leg-spin bowler.

LIBS the Liberal Party.

MACKA'S MacDonald's (either the hamburgers, or the place where they're sold).

MUSO musician.

MYXO myxomatosis (a disease used to kill off rabbits during a serious rabbit plague).

NANA banana (most common among children).

NASHO (1) National Service; (2) a person doing their national service.

NATS the National Party.

NEWBIE a new person.

NEWIE a new device or object or thing.

NIBBLIES snacks, that which can be nibbled on.

NICKO Nicholas.

NING a nincompoop (someone who's not the brightest light bulb in the box).

NON COMPOS non compos mentis (a bit of Latin for a ning).

OBS objections ('anyone got any obs to that?').

OFFIE an off-spin bowler.

OLDS, THE the parents.

OODNA Oodnadatta.

OP SHOP a charity shop, an 'opportunity shop'.

PADDO the Sydney suburb of Paddington (used less often now that it's been gentrified).

PARRA (1) paranoid; (2) the Sydney suburb of Parramatta.

PASH passion, used to indicate someone is feeling romantic (as in 'she has a pash on ...').

PAV pavlova (a dessert of meringue, cream and fruit).

PERISHER Perisher Valley in the Snowy Mountains.

PHYSIO physiotherapist.

PICKY (1) pedantic or excessively choosy or selective, over-fussy; (2) a picture.

PINKO of the political left (obsolete since the downfall of the Soviet empire – since the Russian communists were 'Reds' their local sympathisers were at least a shade of pink).

POKIES poker machines.

POLLIES politicians.

POM, POMMY an English person.

PORKY a lie (rhyming slang, 'pork pies' = lies).

PORT the nearest place with Port in its name (Port Macquarie, Port Augusta, etc.).

POSTIE postman.

PREGGERS pregnant.

PRESSIE (1) a gift or present; (2) a Presbyterian.

PRO a prostitute.

PROBS problems (often used in the positive sense of 'no probs').

QUICK, A a fast bowler.

RANGA person with red hair (from 'orang-utan').

REFFO refugee (now somewhat obsolete, more common in the 1950s).

RELS, RELLIES, RELLOS the relatives.

REZ the Melbourne suburb of Reservoir.

RHINO nineteenth-century slang for money.

RMs boots (abbreviation for RM Williams, legendary Aussie bootmaker and saddler).

ROCKIE Rockhampton.

ROOMIE roommate.

ROTTIE Rottnest Island (Western Australia).

ROUGHIE, RUFFIE a bit rough, either a person or thing that doesn't quite fit in.

SALTIE saltwater crocodile.

SALVOS (1) Salvation Army; (2) Salvation Army officers.

SAMBO sandwich.

SANGER sandwich.

SCHOOLIES a week of unbridled celebration following final exams ('Schoolies Week').

SCRATCHIE a scratch and win lottery ticket.

SEMI a semi-trailer.

SHAZZA, SHAZZ Sharon.

SHONKERS Shanghai.

SICKIE sick leave (often used in a derogatory sense of feigning illness, to 'take a sickie').

SINGERS Singapore.

SINGO Singleton (either the town or any person of that name).

SMITHY Sir Charles Kingsford Smith (legendary Aussie aviator).

SMOKO a break (for morning tea or a smoke or both).

SPAG BOL spaghetti bolognese.

SPEC speculative (as in 'spec builder', who builds a house before selling it).

STAT DEC statutory declaration.

STUBBIES short shorts.

STUBBY a can of beer.

17

SPEAKING STRINE

Television arrived in Australia in 1956, but at first it spread only slowly. As a young boy I remember our first television set (black and white, 17-inch screen) arriving in our house in 1960. So what did we do for home entertainment before the magic box arrived? We listened to the radio. When I was very young there were dramas and serials on radio (hard to imagine today, isn't it?). And from those radio dramas my small mind reached a strange conclusion: that every other country in the world had an accent (either a comical or peculiar one), while the way we spoke in Australia was simply natural, normal – neutral, if you like. In effect, we were accent free and the rest of them had funny ways of talking.

Well, that's the way small children think. Clearly we Australians have our own unique accent – and it's an important part of Aussie English. The New Zealand accent may be similar, but it's still not quite like ours.

So, how did it come about? How did we come to speak like no one else on earth?

In chapter 2 I told the story of how the English language that landed on these shores on 26 January 1788 came from all over the British Isles. There were Cockney, Irish, Scottish, Welsh and Yorkshire convicts. In fact, most of the regional dialects of the United Kingdom were represented among the convicts and their jailers (the military types of the New South Wales Corps). These settlers not only used different dialect words, but they spoke with differing accents – from the rolling r's of the Scots to the lyrical vowels of the Irish to the glottal stops of the Cockneys to all the rest.

The experts tell us that when a bunch of widely differing accents such as these is thrust together (in this case in a remote and harsh land) what happens is a kind of blending. And it's this blending of regional British accents that produced the distinctive Aussie accent. It happens, so they tell us, in three stages.

The first settlers, as they struggle to survive side by side in a tough landscape, modify their accent – they make small changes to how they speak – in order to be better understood by those around them. Misunderstandings bring difficulties all round, so each person tries to speak a little more clearly, less hurriedly, with more careful enunciation. This is how the blending begins. What I'm calling 'blending' the experts called 'dialect levelling'.

And this deliberate modification is the first stage of that process.

The second stage happens with their children. All the evidence shows that children are more influenced in their speech and accent by their peers than by the adults they mix with. So these children are hearing a mixture of modified ('levelled') accents around them, and are speaking to each other in a blend of the voices they hear. This rich stew of levelled accents is being mixed around in a common pot of blended speech – in which all the verbal flavours run together and none overwhelms the others.

Picture it as being like a bicycle wheel with a hub and spokes. We start with a range of widely varying accents (from different parts of the British Isles) arriving as distinctive, and quite different, spots on the hub. In the second generation these differences are sliding down the spokes towards the central hub.

The third stage in this accent development happens in the children of those first children – who are now influencing each other all in much the same direction. This is when the variety of accents we started with (Irish, Scottish, Cockney, Welsh, Yorkshire, Devonshire and all the rest) have lost their distinctions and are sliding all the way down the spokes to a common hub. The process, the experts say, takes about fifty years (or two generations). That means that by about 1840 a recognisably distinct Aussie accent had been born.

Dr Bruce Moore, the former director of the Australian National Dictionary Centre in Canberra, says this process occurred first in Sydney, and from there much the same accent spread around Australia. Bear in mind that the early colonies all spread out from Sydney – first to Hobart, then to Brisbane, Newcastle and then further afield. The colony was, after all, a bureaucratic establishment run by the British military, with strict military control. By the time it became anything more democratic the (more or less) uniform accent had spread across the nation.

The contrast here is with the American colonies, where distinct groups settled in widely separated places and tended to stay there – developing their own local accent. The result is the wide range of regional accents heard across America today, from Tennessee to Brooklyn, and from Texas to California. In Australia we have slight regional variations in accent, but only slight by comparison to the differences between, say, Chicago and New Orleans.

So what did this early Australian accent – that was hopping like a cane toad from place to place – actually sound like? Sadly no one was thoughtful enough to invent sound recording to preserve a specimen, so we have to rely on the reports of British visitors. And what they say is interesting.

One visitor described the sound of the speech produced by all that accent blending as 'a better language, purer, more harmonious than is generally the case in most parts of England'. Surprised? That quote, by the way, comes from James Dixon writing in his *Narrative of a Voyage to New South Wales and Van Diemen's Land in the Ship 'Skelton' in the year 1820*. And other British visitors made similar remarks.

What they were really noticing was the absence of any strong regional British accent. If you take away all the odd regional ways of pronouncing words the result is a kind of 'common English' with the rough edges removed. That's what the visitors were hearing in our accent. And they were calling it a very 'pure' form of English.

Caroline Leakey was born in Exeter, in England, in 1827. She spent five years with her sister in Tasmania (from 1848 to 1853). Several years after her return to England she recorded what she saw and heard in a novel called *The Broad Arrow* (named for the arrow symbol on convict uniforms).

Her description of Hobart (as it must have been around 1850) ends with her comments on the Australian accent. In the following extract she is being escorted by her uncle, to whom she comments that the mixture of retail shops in Hobart reminds her of London. He says she is mistaken: 'Trades from all parts of Britain have settled here. Every county [every region] has its representative ...'

Then he goes on to explain the nature of the Australian accent she is hearing:

To the same cause may be attributed the freedom from peculiarity in the tone and pronunciation of the natives [meaning locally born settlers]. As children they have no opportunity to contract the nasal twang or gutturals of any particular province; by the constant change of servants, and from an intercourse with a diversity of accents, they are preserved from fixing on any one peculiarity. The Irish brogue heard today is tomorrow changed for the broad Scotch accent; the Devonshire drawl soon forgotten in the London affectation; the Somersetshire z's are lost in Yorkshire oo's. [That's the levelling process – and his final remark points to the result.] If you have not already remarked it, you cannot fail shortly to note how very well the common children speak, even when the parents set them no good pronunciative example.

That's where the Aussie accent began – as a better, purer form of spoken English!

But that's not how our accent is regarded today – so what's happened to change things? I'll answer that in a moment, but first: can we guess what that original Aussie accent sounded like? I think we can, and here's my guess.

When I first joined the ABC in 1974 they still ran a three-day 'Induction Course' (how quaint, how old fashioned) to introduce us newcomers to the high standards expected of ABC employees. In that course we were told there were three strands of the Australian accent: Broad Australian, General Australian and Cultivated Australian. (I think the idea at the time was that we should try to speak like 'cultivated Australians'.) My guess, for what it's worth, is that the original Australian accent would have sounded much like General Australian – somewhere in the middle between Broad and Cultivated.

A study done in the 1960s estimated that 35 per cent of us spoke Broad Australian or Ocker (which we'll return to later under the name of Strine), 55 per cent spoke General Australian and 11 per cent spoke Cultivated Australian. And that middle one, General Australian, is my guess as to what our original accent might have (more or less) sounded like. (But until they invent a time machine I can't go back and check it out.)

So how did that original Aussie accent split up into three varieties? And how did the world's opinion change from regarding Aussie speech as 'pure' to sneering at it as flat and horrible?

Here's my suggestion: we fell victim to the Elocution Movement.

This was a movement that arose in the 1700s with the aim

of teaching people to speak well (the name is related to the more familiar word 'eloquence'). Thomas Sheridan (1719–88) was an Irish-born actor and educator (and the father of playwright Richard Brinsley Sheridan). He travelled around the British Isles giving lectures on how to speak clearly and well. In 1762 his talks were collected and published as *Lectures on Elocution*. This was followed in 1775 by *Lectures on Reading* – giving instructions on how to read aloud.

Another actor (presumably also looking for a source of income while 'resting' between plays), a man named John Walker, got into the same racket and produced his two-volume *Elements of Elocution* in 1781. Then in 1791 he published his *Critical Pronouncing Dictionary.*

The Elocution Movement began by mainly focusing on clarity – but over the next century it shifted to a concern not just with clear speech but with 'correct' speech.

To this day linguists talk about RP – meaning 'received pronunciation' – with its implication of pronouncing words 'properly'. From about 1850 onwards the Elocution Movement adopted and promoted 'received pronunciation' (also known as 'standard southern English'), initially concentrating their efforts on the English public school system.

They were now trying to teach us how to talk proper!

This was not English freed from the peculiarities of regional dialects (the Aussie accent had already largely achieved that) – this was one regional dialect (spoken by the educated citizens of southern England) being elevated above all the rest, and being deemed 'correct'. This meant, of course, that all the rest were 'incorrect'. When I joined the ABC this received pronunciation was described as 'the BBC accent'.

But if, as the Elocution Movement claimed, that one way of speaking was right, then anything else – including the Aussie accent – must be wrong. And that's the judgment that begins appearing from the 1880s onwards. Dr Bruce Moore, in *Speaking our Language* (2008), says:

> in the late 1880s, and especially in the 1890s and the first decade of the 20th century, there develops a prescriptivist attitude towards Australian vowels and diphthongs [double vowels] – they are being judged against an 'ideal' or 'standard' pronunciation recently 'invented' in England, and the way Australian English diverges from that putative standard is increasingly noted.

So there you were! For more than fifty years Aussies had been speaking a very pure form of English and then this movement came along and pronounced it impure. The goal posts had shifted.

You can see this in the well-known joke from the First World War. Two wounded soldiers lie side by side in a military hospital behind the front lines somewhere in France. The English soldier moans 'I came here to die', to which the Aussie digger replies cheerfully 'Oh, really? I came here yesterdie'. A gentle, or not so gentle, dig at how Australians were perceived as pronouncing the long 'a' vowel.

So how did we respond to this snooty snubbing of our perfectly good accent? In two ways: some Aussies joined the Elocution Movement and tried to improve their speech, while others thumbed their noses and made their speech even more ocker than before. And that's how the three categories were born that I heard about in my induction course: Broad Australian, General Australian and Cultivated Australian.

We can now see that Cultivated Australian (with its precise consonants and rounded vowels) was, as the name suggested, artificial – deliberately cultivated in elocution classes in schools (certainly in the 'better' schools that aimed to produce the professional class of Australians). So that's where one end of the spectrum came from, but how about the other?

In *Speaking our Language*, Moore suggests that Broad Australian appeared after Cultivated Australian and as a *reaction* to Cultivated Australian. The attitude seemed to be: 'If you're going to bung it on mate, I'll show you just how ocker I can talk'.

Moore reports a 1960s study based on recordings of twelve rural men and women from Tasmania and central-western New South Wales who were born in the 1880s. These are blokes and sheilas from the bush so you'd expect broad ocker accents, right? Wrong! They all spoke General Australian, not Broad Australian. Evidence, I suggest, for my idea that General Australian captures the way our accent used to be before the Elocution Movement split it in three bits.

My impression (and it's only an impression, no scientific research here) is since that study in the 1960s, both ends of the spectrum have been shrinking and the middle expanding. Very few Australians seem, these days, to cultivate a Cultivated Australian voice. Perhaps one per cent? Perhaps even less? While at the other end, regular users of Broad Australian seem to have dropped well below 30 per cent – perhaps to as little as 10 per cent. Just my impression, I admit, but since the 1970s Australia's cultural confidence has been growing, and that includes confidence in the natural middle ground of our speech – the General Australian accent.

If I'm right, most of us are speaking much the way our forebears were speaking 150 years ago, and it's a very pure form of English (so don't let anyone tell you otherwise).

But we can't end this look at the Aussie accent without a special salute to Broad Australian – which many of us will still (deliberately) drop into for comic effect. Personally I find the 'ocker' accent to be as delightfully colourful as wailing, bobbing jazz or blues (if, occasionally, just as discordant).

And in the 1960s this way of speaking was celebrated under the label of Strine. That word, by the way, is the (very) Broad Australian way of pronouncing *Australian*. In this word you go very broad and very ocker by dropping the first syllable of *Australian*, dropping the 'l' towards the end, blurring the final syllable, and turning the middle vowel from an 'a' to an 'i'. That's how *Australian* turns into *Strine*.

The man who drew our attention to Strine was Alistair Morrison. He was born in Melbourne in 1911, studied at the National Gallery of Victoria Art School, and worked for most of his life as a graphic designer (in London and then in Sydney). His 'invention' of Strine came from an incident involving the British novelist Monica Dickens, the great-granddaughter of Charles Dickens.

In 1964 Monica Dickens was visiting Australia on a book promotion tour. Sitting at a table in a Sydney bookshop, signing books for customers, she was approached by an Australian lady who said 'Emma Chissit'. Dickens took the book from the lady's hands and carefully wrote in the front 'For Emma Chissit, with Best Wishes, Monica Dickens'. She returned the book, and the lady looked puzzled.

'No, no,' she said, 'Emma Chissit?'

What the customer was actually doing was asking a question: 'How much is it?'.

When the story was reported, Alistair Morrison began collecting other examples, and he coined the word *Strine* to label this way of speaking. He wrote about his findings in a series of articles in the *Sydney Morning Herald* and then collected his discoveries in a book called *Let Stalk Strine* (translation: *Let's Talk Australian*) and several sequels.

He kept his identity hidden, the books appearing under the by-line of Professor Affabeck Lauder ('alphabetical order' – are you getting the hang of this?) of the University of Sinny (Sydney – see, you can work it out once you've got into the way of reading this).

Some of his observations are simply brilliant. For instance, he tells us that for Ockers a very short period of time is *garbler mince* (you work it out this time). And *baked necks* are what you might have on your breakfast plate on top of the toast. If someone asks you if you attended an event but you missed it you can reply *dingo*. And I love his Strine version of the well-known fairy tale: *Snow White and the Severed Wharves*. Wonderful!

This, then, is our look at the Aussie accent – from the reality of the General Australian that we mostly speak to the fun of Strine. But now it's time to step back into the flow of history and see where the story has taken us. With the help of Sid Baker and John O'Grady we had brought the story through the 1940s and 50s and into the 60s. And that's where we now take up the yarn – looking at the process that led to the birth of the first Australian dictionaries.

WORD LIST

Just a short word list this time – a few of the kinds of pronunciations Professor Afferbeck Lauder calls Strine.

AIR FRIDGE average.

AVAGOODWEEGEND the famous advertising slogan: the Strine version of 'Have a good weekend'.

FORD the opposite of going backwards.

GRADE A a term of general approval, as in 'Donja like this weather? Grade A!'

LAZE AND GEM ladies and gentlemen.

NAW SHAW those suburbs north of the Sydney Harbour Bridge.

SOLD LADY an informal, and impolite, way of referring to one's wife.

STRINE LEVEN our national cricket team.

TERROR SOUSE old dwelling now being gentrified in the inner suburbs.

TRINE a vehicle that runs on rails and stops at railway stations.

18

MAKING
DICTIONARIES

In the year 1966 there was a focus on the Australian language. The movie of John O'Grady's *They're a Weird Mob* appeared in cinemas, the second (and greatly expanded) edition of Sidney J Baker's *The Australian Language* was published, as was Professor Afferbeck Lauder's second collection of Strine, *Nose Tone Unturned*.

Also in 1966 two New Zealand scholars living and working in Australia published landmark books: George Turner's *The English Language in Australia and New Zealand* and Bill Ramson's *Australian English: An Historical Study of the Vocabulary 1788–1898*. Ramson's book was based on his doctoral thesis (which, as it happens, was the first PhD in English awarded by the University of Sydney). A year earlier AG Mitchell and Arthur Delbridge had published *The Pronunciation of English in Australia.*

All this activity was making it clearer than ever that Aussie English needed its own dictionary.

As we saw in chapter 8, Professor Edward Morris had produced his limited *Dictionary of Austral English* in 1898, but he stuck to the more proper and formal end of our language (plus the names of the strange flora and fauna of Australia). Sid Baker's work was monumental, but it was not a dictionary.

Successive holders of the Chair of English Language at Sydney University had been talking about the need for a dictionary of Australian English since the mid-1930s but it remained a dream, not a reality. The dream bubbled on through the mid to late 1960s and into the start of the new decade.

In 1976 Grahame Johnston (Professor of English at the Royal Military College, Duntroon, took Oxford's popular *Pocket Dictionary* and (apparently single-handedly) revised it into *The Australian Pocket Oxford.* He explained that 'Every entry has been scrutinised for its application to Australian conditions.' The result was that the book contained information about our way of life, our political and cultural institutions, some of our characteristic idioms, our games, and our strange flora and fauna.

But this still wasn't the big Aussie dictionary based on a big Aussie word hoard.

So the dream of researching Aussie English and sticking the results in a distinctively Aussie dictionary bubbled on through the 1970s too. But as it bubbled one thing remained unclear: what *kind* of dictionary was needed.

Basically there are two key types: the general reference dictionary and the historical dictionary. The type of dictionary sitting on your desk right now is probably an example of a general reference dictionary. These are the most common, and popular, dictionaries in the world. The general reference dictionary is the fat little book we pick up to consult when we encounter an odd or unknown word. In *Chasing the Sun: Dictionary Makers and the Dictionaries They Made*, Jonathan Green tells us that the earliest English dictionaries were general reference dictionaries (often with a focus on 'hard words').

The seeds of the historical dictionary were, more or less, sown by the great Dr Samuel Johnson with his *Dictionary of the English Language* in 1755 and brought to full flower by James Murray in his magisterial, multi-volume *New English Dictionary* – now known as the *Oxford English Dictionary* (his story is told brilliantly by his granddaughter Elizabeth Murray in her book *Caught in the Web of Words*).

So what's the difference between these two types of dictionaries? If you look up a word in a general reference dictionary it will give the word's meaning (or its several meanings, if it has more than one), sometimes (but not always) an example showing how to use the word, and perhaps a pronunciation guide and a note telling us if it's a verb, noun, adjective, etcetera.

On the other hand, a historical dictionary gives us all that information plus (as its name suggests) the history of the word. It does this by listing underneath the definition(s) what are called 'citations', short quotations showing the word being used. And these are listed historically – from the oldest to the most recent – showing us how the meaning and the use of the word has changed over time.

A short example might explain it best. If you look up, say, the word *fallacy* in a general reference dictionary, perhaps in a compact desk dictionary, you might find an entry along these lines:

fallacy *n*. (1) a false idea or belief; (2) a weakness in someone's argument or ideas which is caused by a mistake in their thinking.

Dr Johnson (and admittedly he was writing back in the 1750s) gives us citations (as illustrations, rather than in historical order) to back up what he says in his more scholarly definitions:

Fallacy *noun*
Sophism; logical artifice; deceit; deceitful argument; delusory mode of ratiocination.

Most princes make themselves another thing from the people by a *fallacy* of argument, thinking themselves most kings when the subject is most basely subjected. *Sidney*

Until I know this sure uncertainty, I'll entertain the favour'd *fallacy*. *Shakespeare*

It were a mere *fallacy* and mistaking, to ascribe that to the force of imagination upon another body which is but the force of imagination upon the proper body. *Bacon*

All men, who see an inch before them, may easily detect gross *fallacies*. *Dryden*

As for the *Oxford English Dictionary* ... well, I won't reproduce it all here, but the entry for 'fallacy' runs to six different meanings or shades of meaning – three of them broken down into (a) and (b) subdivisions – supported, on my count, by thirty-two citations or short quotations, the earliest from 1481 and the latest from 1967.

Every desk dictionary – every ordinary general reference dictionary – has a mountain of citation information in its files. They simply choose not to print it, on the basis that it would be far too much information (much more than the average diction-ary user wants or needs) and they tend to print their definitions in the order of how commonly they are used, not in historical order.

On the other hand, historical dictionaries are published for us word obsessives who want as much information as we can get.

So, those are the two types of dictionaries.

As it turned out, Australia got one of each: first a general reference dictionary, the *Macquarie Dictionary* (in 1981), and then a historical dictionary, the *Australian National Dictionary* (in 1988).

The moving force behind the *Macquarie Dictionary* was Arthur Delbridge, the foundation professor of linguistics at Macquarie University.

As the 1970s began he was invited by the managing direc-tor of Jacaranda Press, Brian Clouston, to edit a distinctively Australian general reference dictionary. At the time, as well as teaching at Macquarie University, Delbridge was chairing a committee at the ABC called SCOSE – the Standing Commit-tee on Spoken English – which published regular guides for

ABC broadcasters on pronunciation and word usage. (On my first visit to SCOSE – as a guest broadcaster – I was delighted to find it was chaired by the legendary Arthur Delbridge. Later, when I became a full member of SCOSE for some years, the chair was that erudite guide to style and language Professor Pam Peters.)

Back in the 1970s Jacaranda Press purchased the rights to an American dictionary called the *Encyclopedic World Dictionary*. The idea was to go through this, entry by entry, and Australianise it, and then add entries covering every distinctive Australian word. A daunting task.

It is the way of dictionary publishing that dictionaries breed dictionaries. So the starting point for this Australian project already had a whole history behind it. The *Encyclopedic World Dictionary* was itself based on Clarence Barnhart's *American College Dictionary*, which was in turn based on the *New Century Dictionary* which was an abridgement of the *Century Dictionary and Cyclopedia* which was an expansion of the *Imperial Dictionary* which was based on Noah Webster's *American Dictionary*.

If that sounds confusing, it's just an indication of how the knowledge base of our language stored in dictionaries grows, is updated, and is adapted to different branches of the English language.

At any rate, Jacaranda Press and Arthur Delbridge began with the *Encyclopedic World Dictionary* and started the long slog of working through it entry by entry, word by word.

Delbridge and his team would meet in the Jacaranda offices in North Ryde, working around a table 'in committee', changing American spellings or expressions and adding Australianisms from their reading, from their experience, and from their perusal of the daily newspapers. Then, late in 1974, Jacaranda Press was taken over by a larger American publishing house and the axe came down on this expensive project.

The tragedy was that the Delbridge team had amassed a vast card file (in that age before personal computers) on the Australian language. This was a valuable data base that could not be wasted. And it was not. Professor Delbridge and his colleagues continued to beaver away in the linguistics department at Macquarie University.

By 1979 Arthur Delbridge, John Bernard, David Blair, Senior Research Assistant Susan Butler (who has since assumed the mantle of editor and publisher) and the rest of the team had something approaching a completed manuscript. At that moment a white knight rode to their rescue in the form of larrikin Australian publisher Kevin Weldon. He had made his money publishing coffee-table books and cook books, and now he established the Macquarie Library Pty Ltd to specialise in publishing Australian dictionaries.

It was Kevin Weldon's money, and his entrepreneurial flair, that resulted in the first edition of the *Macquarie Dictionary* rolling off the presses in 1981. And it continues to roll off the presses (in updated editions) to this day. Despite changes over the years in the publishing house in which it nests, the sixth (revised and expanded) edition appeared in October 2013.

Meanwhile, one member of the original Delbridge team, Bill Ramson, working from his base at the Australian National University in Canberra, had continued to plug away at the idea that Australia needed its own historical dictionary.

In February 1974 Ramson convened a meeting at the ANU which he later looked back on as 'the beginning of the Australian National Dictionary Project'. Following that meeting the process was begun of gathering up citations from Australian literature, historical documents, newspapers and magazines that would form the basis for the entries. The goal was to produce an Australian historical dictionary in time for the nation's bicentenary in 1988.

As this goal was pursued a wrangle developed over who would publish the resulting book. Kevin Weldon, already involved with the *Macquarie Dictionary*, wanted to be the publisher to keep the whole project thoroughly Australian. His rival was the Oxford University Press (Australia). In August 1983 the Australian National Dictionary Advisory Committee held a long meeting at which they decided the publishing contract would go to OUP.

Bill Ramson himself continued to work with Arthur Delbridge's editorial team, and at the same time built up a second team of Australian lexicographers working in Canberra on the ANU campus. By the way, if you haven't come across the word *lexicographer* before, it means 'a writer or compiler of a dictionary'. It comes from two Greek words: *lexicon* (a word list) and *graphos* (write). Dr Samuel Johnson famously defined a lexicographer as 'a harmless drudge'. Actually, what Johnson wrote in his definition (in full) was: 'A writer of dictionaries; a harmless drudge, that busies himself in tracing the original, and detailing the signification of words'.

By 1980 Australia had (and still has) two teams of lexicographers producing two national dictionaries.

Ramson and his team worked under the remote, but

demanding, eye of the Grand Panjandrum of lexicographers, Bob Burchfield, a New Zealander by birth, who edited the great *Oxford English Dictionary* itself for thirty years and was Chief Editor from 1971.

Finally, in the midst of our nation's bicentennial celebrations in 1988 the *Australian National Dictionary* rolled off the presses. It bore the subtitle *A Dictionary of Australianisms on Historical Principles*, and its editor was listed as WS Ramson. It contained some 10 000 words, idioms and meanings that Australia has contributed to the English language. It set out to show the historical development of these words from their earliest use to the present day, supported by some 60 000 dated and referenced quotations drawn from more than 9000 Australian sources.

And having their magnificent databases in place, our dictionary publishers, both Macquarie and OUP, set about producing a wide range of dictionaries – of varying sizes for various readers.

The Macquarie team, for example, in addition to their main dictionary produce a range of titles that include the *Concise Macquarie*, an *Encyclopedic Macquarie Dictionary*, a *Macquarie Thesaurus*, a *Concise Thesaurus*, a *Macquarie Australian Slang Dictionary*, a *Children's Dictionary*, a *Crossword Dictionary* plus (in this electronic age) an online dictionary and an app to load onto your phone.

Oxford, meanwhile, has integrated their Australian database into their general English language database to give us the *Australian Oxford Dictionary*, from which flows a number of offshoots including an *Australian Concise Oxford*, an *Australian Pocket Oxford*, and even an *Australian Little Oxford*, plus the usual special editions for schoolchildren.

Of course the Oxford's major scholarly publication remains

the *Australian National Dictionary*, which the team at the Australian National Dictionary Centre in Canberra have been revising and updating for some time. They tell me we can expect the new edition of their monumental work some time in 2016.

At the same time heaps of other enthusiasts have turned their attention to some sort of dictionary looking at some aspect of Aussie English.

One of the earliest, and most distinguished, among these enthusiasts was Gerry Wilkes, Professor of Australian Literature at Sydney University. In 1978, well before the big dictionaries had appeared, he produced his *Dictionary of Australian Colloquialisms*, with each headword (as it's called) supported by historical citations. In 1984 Stephen Murray-Smith produced his *Dictionary of Australian Quotations*.

Lenie (Midge) Johansen came out with 'a ripper guide to Aussie English' in 1988 which she called *The Dinkum Dictionary*. The same title was chosen by Susan Butler in 2001 (by then she was the publisher of the *Macquarie Dictionary*). But her *Dinkum Dictionary* was rather different, choosing to tell the colourful stories behind a couple of hundred Aussie words.

June Factor gave us *Kidspeak: A dictionary of Australian children's words, expressions and games*. Then I got into the racket with my *Dictionary of Australian Phrase and Fable*.

All of these smaller or more specialised dictionaries (and I've only listed a few) are in addition to the two giants looming over the landscape of Aussie English: the *Australian National Dictionary* and the *Macquarie Dictionary*.

With two national dictionaries regularly bringing out new editions we are, for our size, remarkably well served for dictionaries. So whatever Aussie English does now and in the future we can be certain it will be well tracked and well reported.

And on that note we turn from the dictionary to the atlas. There are two ways in which Aussie words can be 'mapped': one is by being a placename, and the other is by being one of those local words that belongs to a particular region or district. We look at both of these in the next chapter.

WORD LIST

Every time a new edition of a dictionary comes out, what we all look for (and what the news media reports on) are the new words. Here are some of the 'newish' words that have appeared in our dictionaries over the last few years. (The definitions are mine – so don't blame the dictionaries!)

BLOBFISH a slimy pink fish living in very deep water off the coast of southern Australia.

CATTLE CLASS cramped economy class seats on long-haul flights.

DINING BOOM the growth of Australia's farm business in response to a growing Asian middle class wanting better quality food.

ECONOMIC REFUGEE a person claiming to be fleeing from persecution, but whose migration is in reality motivated by money.

FIBRO MAJESTIC a play on the name of the Blue Mountains resort hotel the Hydro Majestic, used as a label for the fibro homes build in profusion in Australia during the first half of the twentieth century.

FIRE-RESISTANT GARDEN a garden using the types and positioning of plants and the choice of materials to slow the progress of a bushfire.

FIRESCAPE landscaping done with the same intention: to reduce the risk of bushfire by using fire breaks, fire-resistant plants and materials and so on.

FISCAL CLIFF the risk of falling into a rapid economic collapse (as can happen to a company or a national economy).

FROGGER a volunteer with Red Frogs Australia (established to provide protection and care during Schoolies Week, in particular from alcohol and drug use); from the red frog lollies handed out by these volunteers.

FUGITIVE EMISSIONS gases that escape when coal is mined or that are released during the industrial production of oil and gas.

GREEN TAPE slow, frustrating bureaucratic environmental checks.

KANGA CRICKET a form of cricket modified for children.

KELPIE SYSTEM a system for rounding up and collecting abandoned supermarket trollies; named for the Australian Kelpie breed of dog which is brilliant at mustering livestock.

MICRO PARTY a single-issue political party with a small support base, needing preferences of other parties to win a seat in the Senate.

MUD ARMY volunteers who help clean up damaged homes (and other buildings) after a flood.

MUMMY BLOG online blog written by a young woman (often to fill in time while on maternity leave caring for a new baby or small toddler).

NIPPLE NAZI one who opposes breast feeding in public places.

ONE-PUNCH LAW a law covering manslaughter committed by means of a (usually drunken) king hit on an unsuspecting victim.

ROO BALL a form of soccer modified for children.

SHOWROOMING examining products in a bricks-and-mortar shop before buying them online.

SLUGGOS Speedos swimwear.

SOCIAL READING a way of sharing the experience of reading an ebook, either by blogging on social reading websites about it, or by emailing selected text to a friend.

STOLEN GENERATION Aboriginal children taken away from their birth parents by well-meaning but misguided officials and placed in foster homes (usual with a white couple) or in children's homes.

WALLA RUGBY a form of Rugby Union football modified for children.

WATCH AND ACT a mid-range bushfire warning.

19

MAPPING
WORDS

Australia is a big place. It has what poet Les Murray calls 'the quality of sprawl'. Everyone who takes their first flight from Australia towards Asia notices how long it takes to pass over the Australian continent – 'it just goes on and on', as a friend said to me. Much of it is empty and largely ochre coloured, with tiny townships dotted at rare intervals – each with its Anzac war memorial in the main street and sometimes more pubs than people.

And, as I've tried to show in this book, this vast, sprawling continent is filled with words – our own special words that belong here more than anywhere else.

There are two ways in which Australian words can hold a

place on an Australian map. The first is as a placename, the second is in the form of a regionalism – an Aussie word that belongs to one part of the map. In this chapter we'll sketch out a little about both of those.

We'll start with regionalisms – expressions that are used in (or originate from) one region of Australia.

Once again we need to note that Aussie English is remarkably consistent around the whole country (much more so than British English or American English). But there are still are some interesting regional variations. This is because Australia began as a bunch of regions – as six colonies that finally voted to become one nation in the 1890s.

The regional origin of the nation of Australia is still obvious. The national domestic cricket competition, the Sheffield Shield, is state versus state. The biggest competition in rugby league is State of Origin. And the (more jokey than serious) Melbourne versus Sydney rivalry is well known.

Out of our regional origins come a bunch of small differences in our vocabulary. Take, for example, the case of the processed meat product known in many places in *devon*. Depending just where you are in Australia the same substance takes on a host of other names – *baron sausage, Belgian sausage, beef Belgium, Byron sausage, Empire sausage, fritz, German sausage, luncheon sausage, polony, pork German, Strasburg sausage* or *Windsor sausage*.

How can a pre-cooked, pressed meat coming out of a smallgoods factory have so many names? Well, some of them may have begun as proprietary names. The German names may have begun in places with many German settlers (such as South Australia) because of the popularity of this kind of sausage in the local community. Then with the outbreak of the First World War there was a move to abolish German-sounding names and replace them with something more patriotic – giving us the *Empire sausage* and the *Windsor sausage*.

And what about the line of poles running down your street carrying the electricity wires? What are they called? Well, it depends where you are. In New South Wales it might be a simple *power pole* but in Tasmania it will be a *hydro pole* because of the hydro-generation of electric power in that state. Elsewhere it might be called an *SEC pole* (from State Electricity Commission) or *telegraph pole* (decades after the telegraph ceased to exist as a form of communication), while in South Australia it is a *Stobie pole* and is made of concrete with sides of steel. This takes its name from engineer James Cyril Stobie (1895–1953), who designed it for the Adelaide Electric Supply Company in 1924 to compensate for the lack of hardwood and the widespread presence of termites in South Australia.

So even though our language doesn't vary across the continent as much as other nations, we do have *some* regional expressions.

At the Sydney Writer's Festival I once sat on a panel discussing regionalisms with poet Les Murray. And he had a wonderful collection from his part of the world (the mid-north coast of New South Wales) to share with us.

Around his way, Les told us, no one says 'please' – instead they say 'I suppose ya couldn't …' And instead of 'thank you' they say 'Good onya!' Les also insists that in his patch of Australia (an old dairying and logging area) no one ever gets fat: instead they 'put on condition'. And if, on the other hand, you've lost weight the locals will tell you that you're looking 'tucked up' or that you've 'fell away a bit'.

The lexicographers at the Australian National Dictionary Centre have started researching this phenomenon and producing a series of books of state regionalisms. So far they've given us: *Words from the West: A glossary of Western Australian terms* (1994), *Tassie Terms: A glossary of Tasmanian words* (1995), *Voices of Queensland: Words from the Sunshine State* (2001) and *Bardi Grubs and Frog Cakes: South Australian words* (2004).

And in case that last one puzzles you, a *bardi grub* is the edible grub (larva or pupa) of either a beetle or moth (the term seems to be used loosely); and the *frog cake* is a small, rich cake, thickly iced (usually in green) with the top of the cake and the icing shaped to look like a frog with an open mouth (the product of Balfours, a famous Adelaide bakery).

For some reason Adelaide seems to be the home of a number of idiosyncratic foods. For instance, there is the *pie floater* – a hot meat pie upside down on top of mushy peas, with a generous dollop of tomato sauce. Then there's the *savoury slice*, a pastry slice with savoury mince filling, topped with cheese and bacon. If you have a sweet tooth, in addition to the frog cake there is the *sinker*, a solid fruit square, with flaky pastry on the top and bottom and topped with pink icing; and the *German cake* – a yeast cake with a crumble topping, sometimes with fruit (either apple or apricot) under the crumble. All are among South Australia's great contributions to the dictionary of Australian gastronomy.

The problem with scholarly lexicography is that it is (in the main) tied to those citations mentioned before. So if an expression hasn't appeared in print it can be hard for the lexicographers to pick it up. And many of our regionalisms remain part of the spoken, not written, language.

For that reason the *Macquarie Dictionary* team tried a different approach. They joined up with ABC Online to run a website called *Word Map* which invited the folk of Australia to contribute expressions heard in their part of the country. The result was overwhelming, with the website having over 20 000 hits a week. (We love our language here in Oz!)

The Macquarie editorial team worked through the thousands of submissions and posted them on the site, inviting comments and feedback. They were looking for items that were more local than general Aussie colloquialisms but were in general currency in a region, not just an expression used in one family. (It's a tricky business, this lexicography.)

When all the filtering had been done by the experts the resulting (thousands!) of regionalisms were handed over to me (by Susan Butler of the *Macquarie Dictionary*), and I was asked to turn them into the first national dictionary of Australian regionalisms. Which I did – a book called (fairly obviously) *Word Map* (2001).

Some of the expressions we reported worked only in one small region. For instance, the *seven o'clock wave* only happens in Wagga Wagga. Except that it doesn't actually happen at all. It's a mythical wave that visitors are told about: 'Hey mate, get out your surfboard – at seven o'clock every evening they open the floodgates on the dam up the river, you can catch a great wave!' Except that you can't, because there isn't one. It's a local joke. But it made it into *Word Map* as a regional expression.

Other expressions that ended up in *Word Map* were more widespread, such as *six and out* – one of the basic rules of backyard cricket (if you hit a ball over the fence you've scored a six and lost your wicket).

Depending on where you are in Australia a wine cask (a plastic bag inside a cardboard box, basically) can have a variety of local names. Some of these actually have a placename in them, such as *Balga handbag*, *Broadmeadows briefcase*, *Coraki handbag*, *Dapto briefcase*, *Dubbo handbag* and so on. Others are more generic, such as *death bag*, *bag of death*, *boxie*, *box monster*, *goon box* or *lady in the boat* (that last one comes from an illustration found on the front of one particular brand of wine cask). And then there's my favourite: *vino collapso* (showing a flash of the old Aussie verbal inventiveness).

Only occasionally will we run into these regionalisms in a way that confuses us. For instance, if you ask an assistant in a department store where you can buy a 'costume' they may send you to the fancy dress section, unless you happen to be in a place that recognises that *costume* actually means *swimming costume* (often shortened to *cozzie*). In other places the same item will be *bathers* or *swimsuit* or *trunks* or *togs*.

So the regional differences are there, and you may occasionally encounter them. But just like the regional variations in our accent, they are minor compared to other English-speaking countries.

The reason for this, by the way, is that almost from the beginning we have had a very mobile population – a mobility greatly increased by the gold rushes of the 1800s. The big sheep and cattle industries also kept Australians on the move. And it was this movement in our population that tended to minimise the differences in our vocabulary and our accent.

And across this widely travelled wide brown land are a bunch of other important words: placenames. I am reliably assured that if you count every name given to every place (even the smallest creek or hill) you'll find more than four million placenames in Australia. I am also told that more than three-quarters of these names are of Aboriginal origin.

For example, in the heart of western Sydney is Parramatta. The name is Aboriginal and is commonly translated as 'the place where the eels lie down' or 'head of waters'. It comes from an Aboriginal word – either *baramada* or *burramatta*. The local people appear to have been called the Burramatta people (*burra* meaning place, *matta* meaning eels) and they belonged to the larger Dharuk grouping.

In that explanation what you notice is the uncertainty. That's because tribes around large cities died out and it was local folklore that preserved what was thought to be the original meaning of an Aboriginal placename. Until around the 1930s there was no really systematic research into Aboriginal languages, and this uncertainty is the result.

The pronunciation and spelling of *Burramatta* shifted to *Parramatta* because of how European settlers said the Aboriginal word. Then, just to make things more confusing, the place we now call Parramatta was originally Rosehill – the name given by Governor Phillip in honour of British bureaucrat Sir George Rose (Secretary of the Treasury, later Secretary of the Navy). There still is a Sydney suburb called Rosehill – the name was shifted down the road a bit when Parramatta was re-christened with its Aboriginal name.

That sort of re-naming has become more common as Australians seek to recognise the original names applied by the original inhabitants. So Ayer's Rock became *Uluru*. William Gosse visited the giant monolith in 1873 and named it in honour of Sir Henry Ayers, who was Premier of South Australia at the time. In 2002 its Aboriginal name was restored – *Uluru* being the name in the local Pitjantjatjara language (and it appears to have no other meaning, except that one, 'big rock').

Something similar happened to the Olgas. In 1872 explorer Ernest Giles visited this remarkable rock formation, and the name Mount Olga was bestowed by Baron Von Mueller in honour of Queen Olga of Württemberg, 'one of the royal patrons of science'. In 2003 it reverted to its Aboriginal name *Kata Tjuta*.

On the other hand, there are bucketloads of Aussie places still bearing the Aboriginal names that local settlers discovered when they arrived, and that have been in use ever since.

For example, the legendary outback town of Gundagai celebrated in song ('The Road to Gundagai') and story (the dog on the tuckerbox, nine miles from Gundagai) has always had its present name, of Aboriginal derivation.

Gundagai is actually an abbreviation of the longer, more complicated word *gundabandoobingee*, which is said to mean 'cut with a tomahawk at the back of the knees' (from *gunda*, 'sinews at the back of the knees', and *bingee*, 'cut with a tomahawk'). If that's the case it might refer to some battle in the distant past. But it's not certain, because that long word might also (so the experts say) mean 'going upstream'. This is all from so long ago that no one now knows for sure.

Or take the case of Canberra, Australia's national capital. Brian Kennedy, in his book on Australian placenames, says Canberra comes from an Aboriginal word said to mean 'meeting place'. But Shane Mortimer, an Elder of the Ngambri people, says the place and the people (the earliest inhabitants) shared the same name. Hence the area where Canberra now stands was originally called *Ngambri*.

But the new settlers in the 1820s found this hard to pronounce so they anglicised it to *Kamberri*. And that's the name that appears on documents from 1832. Then in 1913 Lady Denman, the wife of the then Governor-General, declared the new capital of Australia to be called Canberra. From *Ngambri* to *Kamberri* to *Canberra* – that's the journey. As for meaning, *Ngambri* meant the cleavage between a woman's breasts – the land lies between what are now called Mount Ainslie and Black Mountain.

Other places were named by European settlers either out of bitterness (Mount Hopeless, Mount Disappointment) or from sheer eccentricity. How else can you account for a place called Come-by-Chance?

The name is so eccentric that when Banjo Paterson stumbled across it, he burst into verse:

> As I pondered very weary o'er a volume long and dreary –
> For the plot was void of interest – 'twas that Postal Guide, in fact,
> There I learnt the true location, distance, size, and population
> Of each township, town, and village in the radius of the Act.
>
> And I learnt that Puckawidgee stands beside the Murrumbidgee,
> And that Booleroi and Bumble get their letters twice a year,
> Also that the post inspector, when he visited Collector,
> Closed the office up instanter, and re-opened Dungalear.

But my languid mood forsook me, when I found a name that
took me,

Quite by chance I came across it – 'Come-by-Chance' was what I
read;

No location was assigned it, not a thing to help one find it,

Just an N which stood for northward, and the rest was all unsaid.

And Come-by-Chance is still there – in the Pilliga district of
northern New South Wales. At the 2006 Census, Come-by-
Chance had a population of 187.

A lot of country towns have a small hill, or slope, above
them that is often referred to as a lookout. The one above
Gunnedah is called Porcupine Lookout. This may be another
burst of eccentricity, but it might be because *porcupine* was an
early European name for an echidna.

But for really panoramic views you need to go down the road
a little from Gunnedah to Quirindi, where you'll find the local
lookout is called *Who'd-a-Thought It*. Whoever named that one
was clearly caught by surprise – perhaps by the 'vision splendid
of the sunlight plains extended' that could be seen from that
hill.

'Beyond the black stump' is an Australian proverbial expression meaning very, very far away. But was there ever a real Black
Stump on the Australian map? Well, there are no fewer than
four claimants to the title: (1) Merriwagga, a small township
600 kilometres west of Sydney; (2) Coolah in north-west New
South Wales; (3) Mundubbera in Queensland, and (4) Johnson-
ville in Victoria.

The Merriwagga people base their claim on a bushfire in
1886 in which a bullocky's wife died. Coolah Shire has published

a pamphlet spelling out their claim. They say there was a sheep station in the area called Black Stump Run. And as early as 1829 Governor Darling issued a 'limits of location' proclamation saying land was not to be sold or let or occupied beyond the boundary he set, part of which ran along the approximate location of Black Stump Run. The word 'beyond' to describe land outside that boundary can be found in the *Government Gazette* of 1837. The claim is that the combination of *black stump* and *beyond* establishes the true source of the saying. And it just might.

Finally, the biggest name on the Australian map, the one that stretches from shore to shore in large letters: the name of our country. How did Australia come to be named Australia?

It comes from the Latin *australis* meaning 'southern', and the label *Terra Australis* ('South Land') can be found on early maps. In 1606 Portuguese navigator Pedro de Quiros gave the name *Australia del Espiritu Santos* ('Southland of the Holy Spirit') to all the undiscovered bits stretching to the South Pole. In 1642 Dutchman Abel Tasman called the continent New Holland. Captain Cook also referred to the whole landmass as New Holland, but claimed the east coast and re-named it New South Wales.

It was sailor, navigator and map-maker Matthew Flinders who pressed for the name *Australia* in 1814 in his book *Voyage to Terra Australis*, and Governor Lachlan Macquarie who took up Flinders' suggestion and started using it in his official correspondence. By 1824 the name had caught on, and we've been Australia ever since.

In our story of Aussie English we have now travelled through time, from 1788 to the present day, and we've travelled across the length and breadth of this 'sunburnt land'. Now it's time to look ahead. Perhaps we should climb one of the local hills that a bush town would call a 'lookout' and peer into the future. What do the coming years hold for Aussie English? Where is it going? Is it in good shape? How will the future regard our particular dialect of the English language? That's what we turn to next.

WORD LIST

In this word list we to take a trek across some of Australia's more colourful placenames. Here are just a few of the more interesting ones.

ADAMINABY Aboriginal word: 'camping place', or 'place of meeting'; typical of the many placenames where the exact meaning of the original expression has been lost in the mists of time.

ALICE SPRINGS the original Alice was the wife of Charles Todd, who was in charge of building the Overland Telegraph. Charles got his own place on the map when the sandy (mostly dry) Todd River at Alice Springs was given his name.

ARNHEM LAND Why does a remote bit of the Northern Territory have a Dutch name? It was Matthew Flinders who named the coastline in memory of a Dutch vessel, the *Arnhem*, which got separated from its sister ship on a 1623 voyage to the Dutch East Indies and (accidentally) discovered the coast of northern Australia.

BALMAIN from William Balmain, surgeon on the First Fleet (typical of countless suburbs, towns and streets named after early settlers).

BANANA name of a shire in Queensland (of course), about 100 kilometres south of Rockhampton; it's rich farming country but, no, they don't grow bananas there!

BOOLIGAL Riverina township; from an Aboriginal word the meaning of which has long been forgotten, although local folklore says it meant (1) 'windy place', or (2) 'large swamp', or (3) 'place of flooded box trees'; made famous by Banjo Paterson's poem 'Hay and Hell and Booligal', the joke being that Booligal was so unbearably hot that when you were sent to your just reward you'd prefer Hay or Hell – 'but, Gracious Lord, / Deliver us from Booligal!'

GOVETTS LEAP in the Blue Mountains west of Sydney; the romantic story is that a fleeing convict named Govett leaped to his death there to escape re-capture; the prosaic truth is that Major Mitchell named it after his surveyor William Govett.

HUMPTY DOO near Darwin, this wonderful name comes from a cattle station that used to be in the area, and its origin is disputed: the possibilities are (1) it's a corruption of an Aboriginal word meaning 'popular resting place'; (2) it's just a slang expression meaning everything's upside down; (3) from 'umpty', the army slang word for a dot in Morse Code; or (4) Bill Beatty in *Unique to Australia* says that when the first white settler was asked how things were going he replied, 'Everything's humpty doo', meaning all right.

JERVIS BAY named in 1791 after Admiral Sir John Jervis, the issue here is the pronunciation; there are two rival pronunciations: JARvis (thought to be the way the Admiral pronounced his name) and JERvis (from the spelling); either will do, take your pick.

KISSING POINT not from a Mills & Boon romantic novelette but from the sailor's word for the keel of a ship touching lightly on the sloping riverbed at this point.

LAWSON one of three towns in the Blue Mountains named after the first white explorers to find a path across the Great Dividing Range; the other two are Blaxland and Wentworth Falls.

MOUNT KOSCIUSZKO an Australian mountain with a Polish name? Named in 1840 during an exploration of the Australian Alps by Polish-born geologist Paul Strzelecki after Polish patriot Tadeuz Kosciuszko.

MURRAY RIVER originally named the Hume River in 1824 by the great Australian-born explorer Hamilton Hume; he and William Hovell and their party crossed the river near where Albury stands today. In 1830 Charles Sturt, unaware that he'd stumbled across another bit of the same river, named it after British Colonial Secretary Sir George Murray.

OKAY former copper mining township in Queensland (now deserted) said to have got its name when a jam tin bearing this brand name was found near the mining shaft.

ROOTY HILL not so much a name as an invitation to make

silly jokes; named in 1810 by former British Indian Army officers serving in the New South Wales Corps, from the Hindi name for Indian bread: *rooty* or *roti*.

SEVEN SHILLINGS BEACH said to be the price paid by a Mrs Busby to the local Aboriginal tribe to purchase the use of the beach for herself and family (the transaction is said to have taken place in 1871).

TALLAROOK named after an early pastoral run, and made famous by John O'Hagan's song 'Things are Crook in Tallarook (Since Me Sheila Let Me Down)'.

TIN CAN BAY not an early example of food preserving, but a corruption of an Aboriginal word, *tindhin* (the name of a species of mangrove).

WARRAWARRAPIRALILIULLAMACOUPALUNYA said to be the longest placename in Australia; the Reverend John Flynn, of the Australian Inland Mission, reported collecting this name in the 1930s – the problem is that the Lands Department Place Names Committee of the Northern Territory can find no evidence of its existence!

YARRAWONGA Aboriginal: 'place where the wonga pigeons nested' and the inspiration for a song written by Neil McBeath, a corporal in the AIF in the First World War:

> I'm going back again to Yarrawonga
> In Yarrawonga I'll linger longer
> I'm going back again to Yarrawonga
> Where the skies are always blue …

I'm going back again to Yarrawonga
In the land of the kangaroo.

ZEEHAN another Dutch name on the Australian landscape, this one chosen in 1798 by Bass and Flinders from the name of one of Abel Tasman's ships, and stuck on the map of Tasmania.

20

THE
FUTURE
OF AUSSIE
ENGLISH

Aussie English, in my view, remains resilient, vigorous and lively. You could picture Aussie English as a marathon runner striding along so confidently in the middle of an event that his mind is preoccupied with just where in the house he'll display the gold medal.

Aussie English has a bright future, and shows no signs of carking it just yet.

Not everyone shares my confidence. As I mentioned in chapter 1, in 2006 distinguished Australian journalist Hugh Lunn produced *Lost for Words* – a wail of despair that claimed our wonderful and distinctive language was in its death throes and (probably) beyond resuscitation. Hugh seems to think

Aussie English is the victim of a violent mugging by Hollywood hoodlums. He thinks our language is bleeding and groaning in a dark alley, unable even to provide police with a description of its attacker.

I have debated the future of our dialect with Hugh on radio and I think his mistake is to focus on slang, and even then only on our older slang terms.

The truth is that slang is the fastest changing element in any language. The fact that Australian slang is changing is proof that it's a living language – not a dying one. And, as I explained in the first chapter, slang is only one element that makes Aussie English the distinctive dialect it is.

As far as I am concerned Aussie English is not in the morgue – it's on the beach and the football paddock and the cricket field, and it's still alive and kicking and having fun.

In support of this claim I offer six arguments.

The first is the selective way in which Australians have picked up and employed Americanisms. We keep being told that our distinctive lingo is being drowned under a tsunami of Yankee-speak. And it's certainly the case that the United States sells its popular culture as a 'bulk buy – very cheap' to the rest of the world, including us. But is it killing our language? I think not – because we pick and choose the Americanisms we want to use. The ones we don't like, we don't pick up.

For years Aussies have heard Americans use *in back of* instead of *behind*. It has never caught on here. (In fact, after all these years it still sounds a little odd to Aussie ears.) We've heard Americans (from the movies of the 1930s to the sitcoms of today) talk about *drug stores* – we still call them *chemists*. We've heard the Yanks filling their cars with *gas* for as long as we can remember, and yet we still pump *petrol*. We still run *goods trains* not *freight trains*.

We may debate as to whether 'different *to*' is acceptable, or 'different *from*' is better, but my radar does not detect large numbers of Aussies switching to the American 'different *than*'.

Even useful American expressions for which we have no equivalent are not necessarily picked up and incorporated into our speech.

A good example is *rain check*. When an American on a TV show says 'I'll take a rain check on that', we know they'll take up the offer at a later time. The expression comes from a detachable stub on baseball tickets that could be used for admission to a later game if the current game was washed out. Reportedly invented in the 1880s, I gather such tickets are rarely used these days, but the expression is a permanent part of American English.

It's a useful expression, and we have no equivalent term. Yet it has never entered conversational Aussie English. I gather it was consciously used as part of an advertising campaign by a large retail chain a few years ago – and it *still* didn't enter our language.

Another example would be *milquetoast* – an American expression for a weak or timid person. It comes from a cartoon character named Caspar Milquetoast, created by HT Webster in 1924. It was part of American colloquial speech by 1938, and we have been hearing it for years in movies and TV shows. But, again, it has never really caught on here.

A more recent example would be *hood*, the American rapper's abbreviation of *neighbourhood*. According to some reports, *hood* first emerged from Chicago's South Side in the 1970s. In 1991

John Singleton's movie *Boyz N the Hood* was released, and the word was released along with it. And apparently in American English the word is now gentrifying – it originally referred only to poorer ghettos but can now be applied to New York's Upper East Side.

But despite *hood* being both cool and trendy there is little evidence of young Aussies picking it up and using it as widely as their American cousins. We appear to be very selective as to which Americanisms we allow into Aussie English. These examples (and others like them) are evidence that Australians pick up only those American expressions that appeal to us.

Why we select some terms to adopt and reject others is not clear. There is probably no single reason. In some cases the word was attached to a cultural artefact that does not exist here (such as the ticket stubs called *rain checks*, the Caspar Milque-toast cartoon character and the black ghetto *hoods*). In other cases we were simply satisfied with the word we had and saw no reason to change (why give up *petrol* for *gas*?). Although the reasons vary the fact is clear: we are not the dumb language slaves of Hollywood. And it's difficult to imagine this ever changing.

The most likely future, it seems to me, consists of Aussies continuing to pick up those Americanisms that seem useful, or colourful, while leaving alone other expressions – no matter how common they are in American entertainment.

So the first argument for the resilience of Aussie English is this selectivity.

Secondly, the traffic is two-way. As well as Australians picking up Americanisms, the Yanks also learn how to talk from us. Americans, it appears, have picked up *no worries*, *aggro*, *bludge*,

U-ey and other Australianisms. (Although the 11th edition of *Webster's Collegiate Dictionary* defined *bludging* as 'goofing off'!)

There are various theories as to how this happened. Some experts think it came from the deliberate use of 'Aussie-isms' by American media commentators during the 2000 Sydney Olympics. But Aussie movies, songs and advertisements have also had an impact. As early as the time of the Vietnam War (1962–75), Aussie slang was carried back to the States by American servicemen who'd spent their R&R here, and even before that by American surfers who'd come here for the beaches and the waves.

In 2003 the Disney organisation released an animated movie called *Finding Nemo*, the story of a young clownfish named Nemo who is captured on the Great Barrier Reef and taken to Sydney. The young fish's dad then sets out to find Nemo. One of the animated characters is an Australian shark named Bruce (his voice was provided by Barry Humphries).

As a tie-in with the movie, a small children's dictionary called *Bruce's Aussie Dictionary* was published. This book shows children around the world who loved the movie how to speak 'like a fair dinkum Aussie'. Bruce the Shark (or his alter ego, author Ben Mellonie) tells the kids that someone who's not too bright is a *nong*, walking around with no clothes on is being *in the nuddy* and their *laughing gear* is their mouth. Clearly the export trade in Aussie English is still going strong!

Some people would claim that Australians are providing more new material for the American lexicon than any other country in the world. If Australians can contribute idioms to American English – if the linguistic traffic is two-way – that is further evidence of the resilience of Aussie English.

The third piece of evidence consists of the new verbal inventions Australians are contributing to our conversational lexicon all the time. We may no longer be using *cobber* as part of our everyday speech, but we are constantly coining new and distinctively Australian expressions that display an unending verbal inventiveness.

For example, *blue-tongue* is a still newish slang term for small children (because toddlers are close to the ground like blue-tongue lizards). That expression seems to have been coined in Tasmania. From the Brisbane region comes *desert chicken*, meaning corned beef. From the Central Coast of Queensland comes *muckadilla*, meaning a disorganised person, a messer-about. From the Sydney region comes a nice piece of verbal invention: *YMCA dinner*, meaning leftovers. (It's not a gross calumny on a fine organisation, but an abbreviation of 'Yesterday's Muck Cooked Again'.) And when someone agrees to join in a game or take part in an activity they say they're *thumbs in* for that.

Blue-tongue, desert chicken, muckadilla, YMCA dinner and *thumbs in* – Aussie English is as inventive and linguistically rich as ever.

When English novelist Phillip Hensher was reviewing Tim Winton's novel *Breath* in the British weekly *The Spectator*, he remarked that Australia has the most inventive colloquialisms in the world, and that he would rather be shipwrecked on a desert island with a dictionary of Australian colloquialisms than any other reference book!

On an episode of *QI*, Stephen Fry told with delight the story of taking a domestic flight from Melbourne to Adelaide on which, following the usual safety announcements, the flight attendant said, 'Well, that's enough of that. Now it's time to get some service sliding down the aisle and some scenery sliding past the windows'. That, said Fry, is the way Australians like to play around with language.

It seems to me that verbal invention is a deep feature of Australian culture for reasons which I've already sketched out in this book – and for reasons that go back to the very beginning of the story and the birth of Aussie English from four different sources: English dialect words, the flash language, Aboriginal words and convict–military words. This very word-aware culture then went bush where it flourished and grew as richly and abundantly as tropical plants in north Queensland.

So unless the culture produced by our history is somehow overturned Aussies will go on inventing new locutions – all of them as sparkling as the sunlight on the sea at Bondi!

This constant flow of inventiveness is my third argument for the resilience of Aussie English.

Fourthly, there is flowing quietly beneath the surface of even the most urban and streetwise Aussies a deep reservoir of what I call OBV – Old Bush Vernacular. This reservoir is there to be dipped into and employed (perhaps only occasionally) when the need is felt.

Few Aussies speak OBV all the time. Those who do tend to wear blue singlets, drive utes and listen to John Williamson and Slim Dusty. But for all of us that reservoir is there to draw upon.

When a politician announces something unexpected or challenging they are quite likely (even in the twenty-first century) to tell the gathered media that they are being *fair dinkum*. When they do so they are dipping into this reservoir of OBV.

At the start of the new millennium a London schoolteacher named Mike Coles published a small book called *The Bible in Cockney: Well, bits of it anyway* …. I read his book with delight, and decided that Aussie English was much more fun that Cockney and that we needed the same here. Thus inspired I paraphrased a bunch of the best-known and best-loved Bible stories into our dingo lingo and the resulting small book was published by the Bible Society under the title of *The Aussie Bible (Well, bits of it anyway!)*. It became a bestseller, proving that storytelling in OBV is still popular.

The former Archbishop of Sydney, Dr Peter Jensen, and the former Deputy Prime Minister, John Anderson, both wrote introductions to it. Dr Jensen told me that when he started to read the book he expected it to be nothing more than a novelty, but – to his great surprise – he found that as he read those familiar stories in 'our words' he was moved by them. This language, he concluded, is the language of the heart for many Australians.

This is a man who is an Oxford PhD, and who has spent most of his life as an educator and educational administrator – but still he can find Old Bush Vernacular to be 'the language of the heart'.

It was not so long ago that the members of the Australian Society of Authors voted Tim Winton's *Cloudstreet* Australia's best book. A reading of that novel demonstrates how Winton uses Australian language to deeply move the reader. The anguished, or blunt, or comic utterances of the residents of Number 1 Cloud Street are what I'm calling (for want of another label) OBV.

The *Cloudstreet* example suggestions one possible future for Aussie English: the OBV substrata might cease to be a living tradition, and become a literary tradition instead (learnt in school from Banjo Paterson and Henry Lawson). That's possible – but I don't believe it will happen.

What keeps OBV alive is the not uncommon feeling (among even the most coastal Australians) that our national identity is preserved in the bush. City-living Aussies love such things as bush walking, bush bashing, bush tucker and bush holidays. The heart of Australia lies in the heart of the continent. I can't see time changing that.

So, my fourth argument for the resilience of Aussie English is the reservoir of Old Bush Vernacular that lurks beneath the surface of urban Australia. (Somewhere deep inside that pale-faced, anxious stockbroker in his grey suit is a weatherbeaten stockman in a battered old Akubra.)

And fifthly, there is the role of the next generation.

I'm often told that I speak for a dying generation, and that the next crop of Aussie kids will have no Aussie English, and will speak only a bland (and largely Americanised) form of global English. The evidence is otherwise.

Which brings me back to June Factor – the distinguished Australian folklorist who has had her finger on the pulse of the lore and language of Aussie kids for a good few years now. Her definitive book on Australian children's folklore, *Captain Cook Chased a Chook*, appeared in 1988. Earlier, in 1983, she produced a book of playground rhymes as *Far Out, Brussel Sprout!*. This included an invitation for children to contribute more Aussie playground expressions and so enthusiastic was their response that several more books followed: *Unreal, Banana Peel!*; *All Right, Vegemite!* and the rest.

And then (as reported in chapter 18) in 2000 she gave us *Kidspeak: A Dictionary of Australian Children's Words, Expressions and Games.* This delightful book tells us that Aussie kids are just as likely to say *grouse* as they are to say cool or *awesome.* Aussie kids still know what *gravel rash* is while the phrase would baffle most Americans.

The current crop of Aussie kids, so Factor records, will say *flatten the maggie*s as an expression of surprise. This is an abbreviation of *flatten the magpies* and is clearly related to such OBV expressions as *stone the crows* and *starve the lizards.*

Aussie kids still use *flash* to mean 'overdressed' – an echo of the earlier expression *as flash as a pox doctor's clerk.* Aussie kids still talk about being *knackered* or *flaking out.* And only here (and mainly in Melbourne) are Greeks nicknamed *fish and chips.* The kids are still using *fly cemetery* but they've extended its meaning from a fruit slice to any biscuit made with sultanas, raisins or currants.

The list could go on, but the point is clear – Aussie English is in good hands and the kids are having as much fun with it as ever. In fact, Aussie kids are displaying the same verbal inventiveness their grandparents did – and the source material they're working on is the conversation of their mates and the adults around them, as well as selected bits of imported jargon picked up from the media.

Aussie English is in good hands – the coming generation is looking after it nicely. So the fifth argument for the resilience of Aussie English is its continued (and creative) use by the next generation.

As a sixth argument for the continuing vigour of our language I would add that, in addition to the linguistic departments in all our universities, we have not one but two dictionary centres.

The Australian National Dictionary Centre is based at the Australian National University in Canberra and operates in conjunction with Oxford University Press, while the Macquarie Dictionary Centre has now shifted to Sydney University and works with Macmillan (the current publishers of the range of Macquarie dictionaries).

A useful comparison here is with Canada, a roughly comparable country. There are about 23 million of us and around 35 million of them. Both of us began as British colonies. Both are English-speaking countries.

The *Canadian Oxford Dictionary* made its first appearance in 1998 – while our *Macquarie Dictionary* has been in print since 1981 and the *Australian National Dictionary* appeared in 1988 (seventeen and ten years respectively before the Canadians burst into print).

The *Australian National Dictionary* contains some 10 000 Australian contributions to the English language, while the *Canadian Oxford* boasts of containing '2200 true Canadianisms' – around a quarter of the number of Australianisms found in the *AND*.

From this I conclude that we have one of the richest and most interesting dialects of English in the world – enough to keep all our linguists and both our dictionary centres in business for a long time to come.

When you put all six arguments together, it seems to me that the conclusion is obvious: the future of Aussie English is as bright as a box of budgies and as strong as a Mallee bull!

WORD LIST

At the end of this, the last chapter, there can be no word list because my crystal ball has carked it and I don't know what words will be invented in the future. But the future of Aussie English begins now, and it begins with you. As you hear, or make up (clever you!) a brand-new Aussie expression you can write it in the blank space below. The future of Aussie English is in good hands – it's in your hands!

ACKNOWLEDGMENTS

US President Woodrow Wilson once said, 'I not only use all the brains I have – but all that I can borrow'. To which I add, 'Well said, Woodrow' (if he wouldn't mind me using his first name). That being so, I want to take a page to acknowledge all the brains I've borrowed (and, as you'll see, it's an impressive bunch of brains).

First I need to thank Dr Brendan Nelson and the Australian War Memorial for permission to quote from Charles Bean's explanation of the origin of *Anzac*. John O'Grady, thank you for your permission to quote your father's insights into Aussie English, both in *They're a Weird Mob* and 'The Integrated Adjective'. And my thanks to Dr Amanda Laugesen, Director of the

Australian National Dictionary Centre, both for her delightful and insightful books, and also for her permission to keep pointing towards, and referring to, the treasure trove of our language found in the *Australian National Dictionary*.

There are many longstanding debts I need to acknowledge, and the first of these must be to Susan Butler, the editor and publisher of the *Macquarie Dictionary*. We have been talking to each other, on and off, for many years now about the delights and puzzles of English as she is spoke in these antipodes, and every conversation has been helpful and enlightening. (She also writes and edits great books on the subject!) Then there's Professor Emeritus Roly Sussex, who has always been generous in giving of his time and wisdom on the topic of our language. I've interviewed Roly a number of times on my radio shows (and even filled in for him on his radio shows when he's been on holidays).

My thanks also to Amanda Laugesen's predecessor at the Australian National Dictionary Centre, Dr Bruce Moore. Not only has he proved to be a most entertaining interviewee on my radio shows on countless occasions, but among his many significant books is the pioneering, serious and academic history of the Australian tongue, *Speaking Our Language*. What Bruce did for scholars I have tried to do for that elusive person 'the general reader' (and have some fun while doing it).

Hugh Lunn is a distinguished Australian journalist who deserves my thanks and acknowledgment for being wrong about Aussie English in such a colourful and interesting way. Hugh and I have debated the present and the future of Aussie English on radio. At the end of the debate we each declared ourselves to be the winner (as is only right and proper). Hugh, thank you for putting some fire into my blood with your book *Lost for Words*.

Other books to which I owe a marked debt are Patricia Rolfe's wonderful *The Journalistic Javelin*, the history of *The Bulletin*; Nancy Keesing's *Lily on the Dustbin*; and June Factor's many books, but especially *Kidspeak*.

Then there are the distinguished dead, the writers who captured Aussie English in print. At the head of this queue stands the great Sidney J Baker – and lining up closely behind him are Banjo Paterson, CJ Dennis (and Dennis's biographer Alex Chisholm), followed by Lawson Glossop, Rohan Rivett, AG Mitchell and Alistair Morrison (Professor Afferbeck Lauder of the University of Sinny).

Who else should I thank? I'm sure there are many, but I've reached that age where memory is not quite as accessible as it once was. My friend John once said to me, 'Kel, you know you're getting older when you bend over to tie up your shoe lace and think "Now what else can I do while I'm down here?"' I replied, 'No John, you know you're getting older when you bend over to tie up your shoe lace and think, "Now what did I get down here for?"' I have reached that age. So I hereby issue a general thanks and acknowledgment to everyone who has fed into my understanding of Aussie English over the years, and ask you to grant my dodgy memory a general amnesty.

Of course I take full responsibility for the way I see the story of our language, and none of the blame should be sheeted home to any of the above. But it was their thinking and writing that got me thinking and writing in the first place. Thank you.

BIBLIOGRAPHY

Arthur, JM & Ramson, WS (eds) *W. H. Dowling's Digger Dialects* (Oxford University Press, 1990)

Baker, Sidney J. *The Australian Language*, 2nd edn (Currawong Press, 1966)

Bassett, Jan *The Concise Oxford Dictionary of Australian History* (Oxford University Press, 1986)

Beatty, Bill *Unique to Australia* (Ure Smith, 1975)

Blaikie, George *Remember Smith's Weekly? A biography of an uninhibited national Australian newspaper* (Rigby, 1966)

Bowler, Peter *The Superior Person's Book of Words* (Bloomsbury, 2002)

Bowler, Peter *The Superior Person's Field Guide to Deceitful, Deceptive and Downright Dangerous Language* (Bloomsbury, 2008)

Brooks, Maureen & Ritchie, Joan *Words from the West: A glossary of Western Australian terms* (Oxford University Press, 1994)

Brooks, Maureen & Ritchie, Joan *Tassie Terms: A glossary of Tasmanian Words* (Oxford University Press, 1995)

Burnside, Julian *Word Watching* (Scribe Publications, 2004)

Burridge, Kate *Blooming English* (ABC Books, 2002)

Butler, S, Delbridge, A, Yallop, C, Bernard, JRL, Blair, D, Peters, P, Witton, N (eds) *Macquarie Dictionary*, 4th edn (Macquarie Library, 2005)

Butler, Susan *The Dinkum Dictionary: The origins of Australian words* (Text Publishing, 2001)

Butler, Susan *The Aitch Factor: Adventures in Australian English* (Macmillan, 2014)

Cashman, R, Franks, W, Maxell, J, Stoddart, B, Weaver, A & Webster, R (eds) *The Oxford Companion to Australian Cricket* (Oxford University Press, 1996)

Chisholm, Alec *The Life and Times of CJ Dennis* (Angus & Robertson, 1982)

Chisholm, Alec *The Making of a Sentimental Bloke* (Georgian House, 1946)

Croucher, John S *The Secret Language: The real meaning behind what people say* (ABC Books, 2010)

Dennis, CJ *Backblock Ballads and Later Verses* (Angus & Robertson, 1918)

Dennis, CJ *The Songs of a Sentimental Bloke* (Angus & Robertson, 1915)

Derum, John *More Than a Sentimental Bloke* (UNSW Press, 1990)

Devine, Frank *The Quick Brown Fox: Using Australian English* (Duffy & Snellgrove, 1998)

Factor, June Far Out, Brussel Sprout! series (*Far Out, Brussel Sprout!* 1983; *All Right, Vegemite!* 1985; *Unreal, Banana Peel!* 1986; *Real Keen, Baked Bean!* 1989; *Roll Over, Pavlova!* 1992; *Okey Dokey, Karaoke!* 2005)

Factor, June *Captain Cook Chased a Chook: Children's folklore in Australia* (Penguin, 1988)

Factor, June *Kidspeak: A dictionary of Australian children's words, expressions and games* (Melbourne University Publishing, 2000)

Glover, Richard *The Dag's Dictionary* (ABC Books, 2004)

Green, Jonathon *Chasing the Sun: Dictionary makers and the dictionaries they made* (Henry Holt & Company, 1996)

Green, Jonathon *Cassell's Dictionary of Slang* (Cassell & Co, 1998)

Jauncey, Dorothy *Bardi Grubs and Frog Cakes: South Australian words* (Oxford University Press, 2004)

Johansen, Lenie (Midge) *The Dinkum Dictionary: A ripper guide to Aussie English* (Viking O'Neill, 1988)

Keesing, Nancy *Lily On the Dustbin: Slang of Australian women and families* (Penguin, 1982)

Kennedy, Brian & Barbara *Australian Place Names* (ABC Books, 2006)

Lambert, James (ed) *Macquarie Australian Slang Dictionary: Complete and unabridged* (Macquarie Library, 2004)

Laugesen, Amanda *Convict Words: Language in early colonial Australia* (Oxford University Press, 2002)

Laugesen, Amanda *Diggerspeak: The language of Australians at war* (Oxford University Press, 2005)

Lees, Stella & Macintyre, Pam *The Oxford Companion to Australian Children's Literature* (Oxford University Press, 1993)

Lewis, Chris *The Dictionary of Playground Slang* (Allison & Busby, 2003)

Lunn, Hugh *Lost for Words: Australia's lost language in words and stories* (ABC Books, 2006)

McLachlan, Noel (ed) *The Memoirs of James Hardy Vaux: including his Vocabulary of the Flash Language* (Heinemann, 1964)

Mellonie, Ben *Bruce's Aussie Dictionary* (Puffin, 2003)

Moore, Bruce *Gold! Gold! Gold!: A dictionary of the nineteenth-century Australian gold rushes* (Oxford University Press, 2000)

Moore, Bruce (ed) *The Australian Concise Oxford Dictionary*, 4th edn (Oxford University Press, 2004)

Moore, Bruce *Speaking Our Language: The story of Australian English* (Oxford University Press, 2008)

Moore, Bruce *What's Their Story?: A history of Australian words* (Oxford University Press, 2010)

Morris, Edward E *A Dictionary of Austral English* (Macmillan, 1898)

Morrison, Alistair *Strine: The Complete Works of Professor Afferbeck Lauder* (Text Publishing, 2009)

Murray, KM Elisabeth *Caught in the Web of Words: James Murray and the Oxford English Dictionary* (Yale University Press, 1977)

Murray-Smith, Stephen *The Dictionary of Australian Quotations* (Heinemann, 1984)

Murray-Smith, Stephen *Right Words: A guide to English usage in Australia* (Viking, 1987)

Niall, Brenda *Seven Little Billabongs: The world of Ethel Turner and Mary Grant Bruce* (Penguin, 1979)

O'Grady, John (as Nino Culotta) *They're a Weird Mob* (Ure Smith, 1957)

O'Grady, John *Aussie English: An explanation of Australian idiom* (Ure Smith, 1965)

Oliff, Lorna *Andrew B Paterson* (Twayne Publishers, 1971)

Paterson, AB 'Banjo' *Singer of the Bush: Complete Works 1815–1900, Collected Works, Volume 1* (Lansdowne, 1983)

Paterson, AB 'Banjo' *Song of the Pen: Complete Works 1901–1941, Collected Works, Volume 2* (Lansdowne, 1983)

Peters, Pam *The Cambridge Australian Style Guide* (Cambridge University Press, 1995)

Ramson, WS (ed) *The Australian National Dictionary* (Oxford University Press, 1988)

Ramson, Bill *Lexical Images: The story of the Australian National Dictionary* (Oxford University Press, 2002)

Richards, Kel *Word of the Day 2: Wordwatching* (ABC Books, 2001)

Richards, Kel *Wordwatch* (Pan, 2001)

Richards, Kel *Pocket Guide to Clear English* (ABC Books, 2002)

Richards, Kel *The Aussie Bible (Well bits of it anyway)* (Bible Society, 2003)

Richards, Kel *Word Map: What words are used where in Australia* (ABC Books, 2005)

Richards, Kel *Dictionary of Australian Phrase and Fable* (New South, 2013)

Richards, Kel & Robertson, *Clive Word of the Day* (ABC Books, 2004)

Roderick, Colin *Poet by Accident* (Allen & Unwin, 1993)

Rolfe, Patricia *The Journalistic Javelin: An illustrated history of The Bulletin* (Wildcat Press, 1979)

Rundell, Michael *The Dictionary of Cricket* (Oxford University Press, 1995)

Semmler, Clement *The Banjo of the Bush* (Lansdowne Press, 1966)

Standing Committee on Spoken English *A Guide to the Pronunciation of Australian Place Names* (Angus & Robertson, 1957)

Thorne, Pamela *How Much Can a Koala Bear?: A guide to commonly confused words* (Viva Books, nd)

Wilde, William H, Hooton, Joy & Andrews, Barry *The Oxford Companion to Australian Literature* (Oxford University Press, 1985)

Wilkes, GA *A Dictionary of Australian Colloquialisms*, 2nd edn (Sydney University Press, 1985)

Wilkes, GA *Exploring Australian English* (ABC Books, 1993)

Index